THE TEXAS FOLKLORE SOCIETY

1971–2000

Volume III

THE TEXAS FOLKLORE SOCIETY

1971–2000

Volume III

Francis Edward Abernethy

Carolyn Fiedler Satterwhite, Assistant Editor

University of North Texas Press, Denton

Publications of the Texas Folklore Society LVII

Printed in the United States of America

First edition, 2000
Requests for permission to reproduce material from this work should be sent to:
Texas Folklore Society
Box 13007, SFA Station
Nacogdoches, Texas 75962

Library of Congress Cataloging-in-Publication Data

Abernethy, Francis Edward.
Texas Folklore Society

Publications of the Texas Folklore Society ; 57

Includes biographical references and index.
Contents: v. 3. 1971–2000
1. Texas Folklore Society—History. 2. Folklore—Texas—History—20th Century.
3. Folklore archives—Texas. 4. Texas—Social life and customs. 5. Texas—History—20th Century. I. Title. II. Series: Publications of the Texas Folklore Society ' no. 57, etc.
GR1.T4 no. 57, etc.
390 s
92-12273
398'.06'0764
ISBN 0-929398-42-4 (v. 1)
ISBN 0-929398-78-5 (v. 2)
ISBN 1-57441-122-5 (v. 3)

Cover art and illustrations by Charles Shaw.

Table of Contents

CORRER DEL PAISANO

Texas Folklore Society

FOUNDED 1909

P. O. Box 13007
Nacogdoches, Texas 75962-3007

January 14, 2000

Paisanos:

The best work that a future TFS Secretary-Editor can do for the future and the welfare of the Society is to take this three-volume history of the Texas Folklore Society and boil it down to one readable volume.

Honestly and truly I did not begin this project with the idea of writing the TFS history in three volumes. I envisioned a moderate sized book that future interested persons could turn to in order to learn more about the continuity of this Society. But my plans came apart at the beginning. I got so involved with Lomax and Payne and that first fall that they got together to begin planning that the most minute details of the TFS beginning took on significance that I felt that I could not neglect. I saw the UT campus and the game and the people and what they wore and what they were singing and reading about so vividly that I could not leave it out. And once I had set a precedent, I enjoyed the research into those times and people so much that the whole thing grew like a yeast. Researching and writing volume I was sheer pleasure. Volume II was enjoyable, but I began to lose aesthetic and historical distance between the happenings in the Society and myself.

This volume III was the hardest to write. The years were so close to me that I viewed them personally rather than historically. And I was very self conscious of using the personal "I" so much—and shifting back and forth between first and third person. I was always self conscious when I had to quote myself. And if I could have found anyone else to write this 1971 ff. story I would have put him or her on it. But nobody knows as much about the people and places and happenings of the last thirty years as I do. The Society has been the focus of my professional life since 1971. Not a day has passed that I have not been concerned with it and its paisanos. So I am the one to do this.

So, what you will notice about volume III of this history of the Texas Folklore Society is that it is a twenty-nine year newsletter from the Society's editor to the paisanos. The chapters are divided according to presses and publications, as much for equal time's sake as for their importance in the Society welfare. I hope that I have not left out too many significant people and important happenings.

Volume one of the history of the Texas Folklore Society was a tribute to our TFS grandfathers—John Lomax, Leonidas Payne, Frank Dobie, and their peers. Volume two recognized our folkloric fathers—Mody Boatright, Wilson Hudson, Martin Shockley, and their kin who taught us the way that we must go. Volume three is the history of a generation who came in wet behind the ears in academic folklore, became the fathers and movers and the shakers of the Society, and now find themselves as the grandfathers, watching a whole new world being created as they move to the sidelines. The process is as natural as birth and death.

The absolute and unquestionable pinnacle of my professional career has been my association with the Texas Folklore Society and its members. The Society has given me, as a member and as an officer, opportunities that I could never have had elsewhere. And its members have given me friendship and an education of a lifetime. I have prized both for forty years.

In your service,

F. E. Abernethy
Secretary-Editor

To James W. Byrd (1925–2000),
who represents our generation.

Jim Byrd was born in the Roaring Twenties, raised in the Depression, came of age on the battlefield in World War II, was educated on the GI Bill, marched for desegregation, joined the Texas Folklore Society in 1960, and spent forty-five years of his life as a much loved and respected teacher of literature and folklore.

GEORGE KITTREDGE
J. FRANK DOBIE
MODY BOATRIGHT
JOHN LOMAX
WILSON HUDSON
LEONIDAS PAYNE
F. E. "AB" ABERNETHY

THE TEXAS FOLKLORE SOCIETY

1971–2000

Volume III

Secretary-Editors of the Texas Folklore Society

J. Frank Dobie (1888–1964)
1922 to 1943

Mody C. Boatright (1896–1970)
1943 to 1963

Wilson M. Hudson, 1963 to 1971

THE STORY IN THE PREVIOUS VOLUMES—

The Texas Folklore Society was sixty-two years old in 1971. It had come into existence under the hands of John Avery Lomax and Leonidas Warren Payne in 1909 at the instigation of George Lyman Kittredge of Harvard. Kittredge had told Lomax to form a branch of the American Folklore Society in Texas, and John did just that. The Society got off to a strong start and had regular, well attended meetings until it shut down in 1917, during World War I.

The Society lay dormant for five years and might have expired had not J. Frank Dobie come along with an ambition to do for Texas legends what John Lomax had done for Texas folk songs. Dobie took the reins in 1922, called the meetings, established a publishing program, and became the driving force behind the Texas Folklore Society for the next twenty years. The Dobie years of the Texas Folklore Society, from 1922 to 1943, were the brightest in the Society's life. J. Frank Dobie was a focus of interest in Texas history, folklore, and culture for Texans generally. He was a nationally known writer, speaker, and teacher, and he shared this fame with the Society.

Dobie turned over the direction of the Society in 1943 to Mody Coggin Boatright, his associate editor since 1937, and left the University of Texas for the University of Cambridge, England. Although Dobie attended TFS meetings periodically, was always feted royally, and remained at the center of Society interest, he was never again an active part of the Society even though he was a continual influence.

Mody became the secretary and the editor for the Society in 1943, the year that the Society was forced to suspend meetings to aid the efforts of World War II—to save tires, gas, and public-transportation space. This was a critical time in the Society's history, and had Mody not been on hand to continue Society correspondence with members and to continue the publishing program, the TFS might easily have passed quietly away. Mody guided the Society through the war and called the members together again after V-E and V-J Days.

During Mody's tenure as secretary-editor folklore was becoming accepted in academe, and much of Mody's work and the work of the Society concentrated on scholarly studies of folklore instead of field collecting. During his time Mody edited three publications by himself and eight more with help from Donald Day, Wilson Hudson, and Allen Maxwell. He turned over the editorial program to Wilson M. Hudson in 1963 but did not formally retire as secretary until 1964.

Wilson Hudson, the Society's editor from 1963 to 1971, became associated with the Society when he began teaching at The University of Texas in 1946. His continuing and growing interest in work in folklore soon made him an integral part of the Society, and when Mody left the campus for a year in 1950 Wilson was put in charge of the next Society publication, which was to be *The Healer of Los Olmos* (PTFS 25–1951). In *The Healer* Wilson made a significant addition. For the first time, tale-types and motif numbers were included, a practice which Wilson was to continue after 1951, during his time as associate editor and after 1963 as editor. During his tenure Wilson edited five PTFSs and five books of popular field folklore in his Paisano Series of the Society's supplementary books.

Wilson's finest contribution to the Society and to folklore generally was his inspiration and direction of James Bratcher's *Analytical Index to Publications of the Texas Folklore Society*, which the Society brought out in 1973. Mr. Bratcher indexed thirty-six volumes of the Society's publications according to tale type, motif number, ballad number, tale synopsis, and finally alphabetically.

Dick Underwood's paisano

I
Getting Started in a New Land—The Encino Years: 1971 to 1978

"I can't get no
sa-tis-faction ?!!!
1776★HAPPY 200
BIRTHDAY AMER-
ICA★1976★★★

1971

Ralph H. Houston (1910–1989)
President 1970–71 at San Antonio
Head of the Department of English and Dean of Liberal Arts at Southwest Texas State University, San Marcos

Wilson announced his retirement in his February 12, 1971 newsletter:

"For several reasons I must give up the secretary-editorship, which I have held since 1964. I can no longer give it the time it requires and carry on research for myself. My eyes, which have been giving me trouble since last Easter, will not stand up under the strain of editing and proofreading. Whoever becomes the next secretary-editor should be assured of institutional and departmental support so that he can have at least a half-time, permanent secretary and be relieved of teaching to the extent of being able to devote twenty hours a week to the work of the Society. His secretary must be a mature, professional typist who understands filing and simple accounting, and she should be employed on a 12-months basis. Part-time students won't do; they aren't skillful or responsible enough and they don't stay long enough to learn the work. Most of the time that I have been secretary-editor my teaching load has been two classes, and I have spent several summers working for the Society and not teaching at all. It is possible, by pushing hard in the long session, to make the summer into a kind of holding operation, provided that the helper in the office is competent and trustworthy.

"Since J. Frank Dobie took office in 1923, the secretary-editor has provided continuity for the affairs of the Society. The new secretary-editor should be willing to remain in office for some years, at least four, I should say. Being aware of the importance of the secretary-editorship, President Ralph Houston has appointed the present councilors and directors to serve as a nominating committee to report at our meeting. I am one of the directors, but at my request I am not to be a member of the committee. If you have any suggestions, please make them to the chairman, E. Hudson Long of Baylor University."

President Ralph Houston appointed the incumbent directors and councilors as the nominating committee. The committee nominated F. E. Abernethy on the assumption of support by the Stephen F. Austin State University, and its President Ralph Steen wrote his letter of acceptance to this editor on March 24, 1971: "If the Texas Folklore Society selects Stephen F. Austin State University as a base of operations and names you as Secretary-Editor, the university will assist in the following ways: (1) by giving you released time from one class in the fall semester, spring semester, and one summer term of each year; (2) by providing you with a part-time secretary; (3) by providing you with office space."

Ralph Steen's terms were accepted, and I became the secretary-editor of the Society, and the headquarters were moved to Stephen F. Austin State University in Nacogdoches. The following is from the preface to *Observations and Reflections* (PTFS 37–1972):

"We moved during the burnt-out end of August, Wilson and I, in the midst of posting final grades, campus construction, and a quiet sadness. We sweated and cussed some as we packed the Society's materials in cardboard boxes and carried them out to the station wagon parked behind Parlin Hall. We took down the pictures of Lomax and Payne and Thompson and some Cisneros sketches that had been used in *The Healer of Los Olmos*. Frank Dobie's old felt hat with a turkey feather in the band was sitting on a filing cabinet, so we put it in. Very gently we loaded a box of Mody's paisanos, five or six of them. Wilson had deposited much of the early correspondence in the State Archives, but several boxes of old programs, advertisements, letters, and brochures remained as relics of our ancestors and of our beginnings. And there were the Society's publications, more than thirty of them that stretched back to Stith Thompson's Volume I in 1916. These make up our umbilicus, the visible chain of the Society's being, that makes us all a part of it from its inception in 1909.

"The Texas Folklore Society is now headquartered on the Stephen F. Austin State University campus in Nacogdoches. I have hung the pictures, shelved our volumes, and filed the materials of our business. Our offices are in the basement of one of the campus' original buildings. Our quarters aren't new and shiney, but then neither are we. The building, named after Thomas J. Rusk, is appropriately solid and comfortable, and the campus is located on the old Rusk homestead. The pines reach tall to the sky here, and their roots grow deep in the red dirt. This part of the country has been Texas for a long time, and its history and traditions form a fitting setting for the Society's headquarters."

The editor officially began his tenure on August 16 and hired Mrs. Martha Dickson as the Society's secretary for what would prove a long and profitable season, ten years. Edwin W. Gaston of Nacogdoches agreed to act as the Society's treasurer, in case we needed a treasurer's signature or his sagacity. The Society's finances, however, were maintained by the secretary-editor and his secretary.

The three immediate problems that faced the new office were financing, book distribution, and office space.

The Society's finances were always a cause of concern. When I assumed office the Society had 368 dues-paying members and a balance of $4047.63. The Society was responsible for publishing a book a year, the cost of which ran around three to four thousand dollars. Our income and outgo was virtually the same. The most frugal of organizations would suffer under such a budget. As a result, at the 1972 meeting we raised the dues from $5.00 a year for individual membership to $7.50. It pained me to be the instrument of that increase, but it was necessary for survival.

The Society had long had problems with book distribution. One of the reasons that Wilson had left SMU Press was that SMU could not get the books out on time. The situation did not measurably improve when he moved to Bill Wittliff's Encino Press. *Hunters and Healers* (PTFS 35), the book for 1969 was not mailed from Encino until late in 1971. *There Was a King in Ireland* (ExB–14), the University of Texas Press book for 1970 was mailed from the press *without a return address* in January of 1972. And *Diamond Bessie & the Shepherds* (PTFS 36) the book for 1971 was not mailed from Encino until the spring of 1972. I sent my first edited PTFS, *Observations and Reflections* (PTFS 37) to Encino Press in April of 1972, with the fond but foolish hope that I could get publications back on a Swiss railroad time schedule.

Space was another problem. I occupied a long, narrow office, a large part of which was filled with an elevator shaft. I preferred this space to the new offices the department was moving into in 1968. I converted the elevator shaft into a darkroom—with the old elevator still hanging like a sword overhead. I needed still more space for the added paraphernalia and responsibilities of the TFS, so late one afternoon I moved a book case and began operating on an office wall that butted against a stair well. With a trusty star drill and a three-pound sledge hammer I proceeded to knock a hole big enough to shine a light and see through. I discovered as much space under the stairs as there was in my office. The result was that I asked President Steen to have a door made into the area and the wall paneled, which he did and which I used as the TFS secretary's office and layout room for many years. Three presidents later, I was informed that the use of such under-stair space violated some sort of state code.

As soon as the Society's office was set up in the fall of 1971, I began work on my first PTFS. Always looking back to Frank Dobie, I took its title, *Observations and Reflections,* from a Dobie essay. I called on all my favorite writer friends for contributions.

Thus began year one for this editor in this new-old East Texas setting. It would be the ultimate experience of his professional life.

1972

Bessie Pearce (1915–1997)
President 1971–72 at College Station
Professor of English and Assistant Dean of San Antonio College, served overseas with the American Red Cross during WWII

And if anybody ever asks me about what happened in 1972, my recollections would be of my first year as secretary-editor of the Texas Folklore Society, not that Richard Nixon smothered George McGovern in the November presidential election and went to Beijing and established ping-pong diplomacy with our sworn enemy, China—nor that Bob Woodward and Carl Bernstein broke the Watergate scandal that year. I could be prompted to remember that in spite of Henry Kissinger's promise that the Vietnam war was nearly over, it was still there, and that Jane Fonda was criticizing American bombing in broadcasts from Hanoi. Oh, yes, now I remember!

Meanwhile . . .

I mailed my first official January TFS newsletter on a copy of Wilson Hudson's TFS letterhead, with the necessary address change, of course. By the time of the June newsletter which included the Easter meeting's minutes, I had written Betty Boatright and had her draw her roadrunner for the Society's letterhead. We have been using it ever since, and Betty's original is hanging in our office.

The Society held its fifty-sixth annual meeting at the Ramada Inn in College Station, March 30 through April 1. Bessie Pearce (nee Elizabeth Melvina, 1915–1997) of San Antonio College presided, and the Aggies own Sid Cox was both local arranger and program chairman. Bessie was a charming, gracious, and strong-willed person who left no doubt that she was president during her tenure. She worked for the Bureau of Censorship in WWII and was cited for her assistance in uncovering a spy ring. Toward the end of the war she served the American Red Cross overseas, probably in the front lines. Bessie was a formidable lady who left bruises when crossed, "he says, from first-hand experience."

Members toured nearby Washington-on-the-Brazos Friday afternoon, and J. Mason Brewer (1896–1975) delivered a delightful banquet address in rhymed, iambic pentameter couplets Friday night. His topic, "I Knew Them All," consisted of character sketches of early TFS members. Mason had been associated with the TFS since 1932, when Frank Dobie discovered his talent with Negro folk tales and published Mason's "Juneteenth" in the 1932 TFS annual. Mason went on to become a well known author, lecturer, and university professor, and the first African-American Vice President of the American Folklore Society. In 1972 he had returned to Texas and was visiting professor at East Texas State University in Commerce, working in Negro folklore with Jim Byrd.

The most important business of the 1972 meeting was the Board of Directors' announcement that Wilson M. Hudson was made a Fellow of the Texas Folklore Society. Wilson would join John Lomax, Leonidas Payne, Frank Dobie, and Mody Boatright as one of the great contributors to the spirit and vitality of the Texas Folklore Society.

Bessie Pearce had presented Wilson Hudson's name to the Directors on February 6, 1972, and had suggested that he be so honored at the College Station meeting that spring. Treasurer Edwin Gaston wrote her that because Mason Brewer already had the center stage at the College Station meeting we should announce his election then but confer it with the proper solemnities and celebrations at the Laredo meeting in 1973. It was so ordered.

Oddly, when Bessie wrote to Wilson (March 21, 1972) merely inquiring about the Society's conferring of fellowships, Wilson wrote the following reply:

"I think there are only two Fellows of the Society. Mody thought Payne had been made a Fellow, but I never ran across any record of this in my files. Mody and I—when he was secretary-editor and I was helping him—decided it was time to make Dobie a Fellow [in 1961, ed.], and we checked with the president, vice-president, and councilors before going on. I decided that Mody should be a Fellow [in 1965, ed.] and checked with the officers—no need to consult directors or Paisano advisers. We gave Dobie a dinner and Mody too, with speakers. We made an occasion in each case. The Society has been very slow to confer its highest honor, and there is fitness in restricting it to the two men who have done the most for the Society."

Democrat that she was, Bessie disagreed with Wilson's not conferring with directors and wrote in the margin of his letter, "Wilson liked to save stamps!"

And it is interesting that Wilson—and Mody—did not know that John Lomax and Leonidas Payne had been made Fellows in 1941. But Wilson was teaching at the University of Chicago at the time and did not come to the UT faculty until after the war, in 1946.

For the record, the following is from Frank Dobie's minutes of the 1941 meeting (see TFS I, 263).

"In order to honor individuals who have done outstanding work for the Texas Folk-Lore Society and in the field of Texas and Southwestern folk-lore, the Society voted to make John A. Lomax and L. W. Payne *Fellows,* it being understood that other names may from time to time be elected to the list."

As mentioned earlier, members received a spate of books in 1972. Myles Dillon's *There Was a King in Ireland* (ExB–14) arrived in January and consisted of five Irish tales that were collected and translated by Professor Dylan of the Dublin Institute for Advanced Studies. The book was beautifully illustrated by José Cisneros of El Paso. Wilson had planned originally to include *There Was a King* in the Society's Paisano Series, which was published by Encino Press but changed his mind when the University of Texas Press agreed to publish it for the Society.

Wilson got *Diamond Bessie & The Shepherds* (PTFS 36–1971), a traditional folklore miscellany, to the press in late 1971, and Bill Wittliff mailed it from Encino Press in the spring of 1972. This was Wilson M. Hudson's last PTFS, and he bid members adieu in the foreword:

"The time has come for me to say good-bye as secretary and editor for the Society. In the summer of 1951, while Mody Boatright was teaching in California, he asked me to edit *The Healer of Los Olmos,* and I did so. When he returned he invited me to join him and Allen Maxwell of SMU Press in preparing our annual volumes. Upon Mody's retirement in 1964 I was chosen to succeed him as secretary and editor. I have tried to carry on in his spirit and in the spirit of his predecessors, J. Frank Dobie and Stith Thompson. In the span from 1951 to 1971 I have edited or assisted in editing thirteen Publications for the Society, and I have edited the five books in the Paisano series. A translation of five Irish folktales, neither a Publication nor a Paisano, which I am now seeing through the press for the Society, will carry no designation of editor. Because I wanted to complete some books and projects of my own, in the spring of 1971 I asked to be relieved of my duties. It seemed to me that I had served my turn. At our last meeting, Francis E. Abernethy of Stephen F. Austin State University at Nacogdoches was elected secretary-editor. I hereby surrender to him, most willingly and confidently, these offices. He will know how to make the most of the ability and vitality inherent in the Texas Folklore Society, which has flourished since its foundation in 1909 and will continue to flourish for many a year."

I started work on *Observations and Reflections on Texas Folklore* (PTFS 37–1972) in the fall of 1971. I was bound and determined to publish a previously unpublished Frank Dobie article and found some of his newspaper articles on deer hunting—"Observations and Reflections on Deer Hunting." Bertha McKee Dobie very kindly edited her husband's series down to one article and sent me what became the lead story and the basis for the title of this first publication. I sent requests to my favorite folklore writers and friends and filled out my first publication with what I thought were exciting folklore articles. Then I called on the talents of Jim Snyder, a young SFA art professor who kept his horses in my pasture and was working on a ranch near Cody, Wyoming. He illustrated the book with pen-and-ink sketches of western art. I loved the meat of that book and the way that Bill Wittliff laid it out. I cannot remember a happier editorial experience than putting together *Observations.* And I still do *not* like the title.

As tacky as it is to quote one's self, the following were my introductory remarks over twenty-five years ago to the membership and to the Publications of the Texas Folklore Society:

"As the new man on the job, I guess I ought to present some credentials. Although I was born in Oklahoma, that area was Greer County, Texas, when my grandparents settled there. Since those first few months as an Okie I've lived in the Panhandle dust and the Gulf Coastal swamps, five miles from the nearest mailbox and in the middle of Big D. I began to consciously think Texas during the centennial year of '36, and thereafter my education was liberally seasoned with my own Texas Trinity—Dobie, Boatright, and Bedichek.

"I shall do my best to keep the lid on my Texas chauvinism, but I am foolish about this state. It has blessed me bountifully in spirit and in store and I love it, head to toe, fingertip to fingertip. . . .

"This does not mean that I view folklore as an exercise in regionalism or provincialism. I do not. Nor do I view it as a snug nest to curl up in to retreat from the cold, sharp edges of the present. To me folklore is the ultimate, all-encompassing field of study. I see a decade, a millennium, or an age go by, but the creature man remains the same, activated by the same urges, responding in the same way as did his ancient cave-dwelling ancestors. Only the symbols change. The gods shift their shape but continue to answer to the same needs, and folklore is the demonstration of this eternal kinship. A single seed contains the essence of all life, and the Texas and Southwestern folklore in this volume contains the essence of universal phenomena. The time and the place and the people happened in Texas, but the hunters and fighters and singers of songs are universals, representatives of the repetitions of history and the everlasting oneness of man."

I dedicated that volume to Wilson M. Hudson, to whom I owed the most.

Bill Wittliff printed two thousand copies of *Observations* and initially bound 1025 copies, 425 of which were sent to TFS members. The cost of printing and binding was $4,366.39, and the market price of the book was $7.95. The Society's balance as of January 1, 1972, was $4,047.63. We added the spring dues to that, but the working capital did not inspire financial confidence.

I had considerable correspondence with Frank Wardlaw at the University of Texas Press during the spring. We were trying to work out publication agreements for Myles Dillon's *There Was a King in Ireland,* the book that became *Mody Boatright, Folklorist,* and Jim Bratcher's index to the publications of the Texas Folklore Society. Frank was also interested in publishing the Society's annuals (Wardlaw to editor, January 31, 1972). I was also interested in that possibility. By April 3, 1972, Frank had received word from his Faculty Advisory Committee that the TFS publications and Bratcher's index were too regional for a UT Press market. But the results of our discussions were the eventual publications by UT Press of the Myles Dillon and Mody Boatright collections.

So, in the artistic world *Grease* played to packed houses on Broadway, Helen Reddy amused one-half of the population singing "I Am Woman," *The French Connection* won the most Oscars, and the TFS published *Observations and Reflections.* I think there is a disparity here, but it is hard for me to recognize.

The editor with Martha Dickson, office secretary from 1971 to 1981

1973

Sidney S. Cox (1910–1980)
President 1972–1973 at Laredo
Professor of English at Texas A&M for twenty-eight years, received the university's Distinguished Service Award, wrote "The Home Place"

After over 56,000 American casualties, the U.S. and Vietnam finally signed a cease fire agreement in early 1973 and guaranteed the autonomy of South Vietnam. We were tired, sad, and embarrassed by the whole mess of Vietnam and wanted out at any cost. Some prisoners of war were repatriated, but many of the military were still missing. Tony Orlando and Dawn sang "Tie a Yellow Ribbon 'Round the Old Oak Tree" in the Cotton Bowl at Dallas, and the song became the POW/MIA song for all those who disappeared in the jungles of Asia. We are still tying yellow ribbons around trees to welcome servicemen back from wars.

The whole nation was dragging itself through the mud of Watergate, and every day's news was deadened by firings and resignations in the Nixon inner circle and the battle over President Nixon's White House tapes and his logs and diaries.

And that was the year that the Supreme Court passed Roe versus Wade and legalized abortion.

But there was a brightness and an excitement in 1973 as members gathered April 19–21 at La Posada Inn in Laredo for the fifty-seventh annual meeting of the Society. Top-dollar hotel room rates for doubles that year was twenty to twenty-six dollars; regular rates were half that. Sid Cox (1910–1980) of Texas A&M was president, and Orlan Sawey of Texas A&I was program chairman and local arranger.

Sid Cox was a distinguished professor of English for twenty-eight years at Texas A&M. Most Society members count as one of the classic presented papers Sid's "The Home Place," which he gave at the Wimberly meeting in 1970 and which is included in *T for Texas* (PTFS 44–1982). Sid was born in a log house near the Blanco River and raised on "the home place" in Blanco County. He was buried on his home place in 1980.

The main business of the Laredo meeting was President Cox's presentation of the fellowship scroll to former secretary-editor Wilson M. Hudson of The University of Texas. Wilson had been inducted as a Fellow of the Texas Folklore Society in 1972, but he was not officially installed until the Friday night Laredo banquet. The membership hailed Wilson as a jolly, good TFS Fellow, and he gave his acceptance speech, "Amateur and Professional Folklorists," later published as the preface to *Some Still Do* (PTFS 39–1975).

Wilson was sensitive to the fact that the Society was made up mainly of amateurs, and he accepted *most* of the results of their folklore interests. But Wilson himself was a true scholar and academician. Thus, we have his inclusion of the classic tale-type and motif numbers in all of his publications. Wilson began his speech with his definition of amateur and professional folklorists and concluded that main part of his speech with illustrations of amateur and professional folklore scholarship among the giants of the folklorists: Bishop Percy, F. J. Child, G. L. Kittredge, John Lomax, Frank Dobie, and Stith Thompson. Wilson was very conscious of Dobie's non-academic stance and felt that Dobie was looking over his shoulder when he was publishing the Society's business. Nevertheless, Wilson's conclusion left room for all of the members of the Society, whom he had led from 1951 and *The Healer of Los Olmos* (PTFS 24–1951) to his retirement in 1971. Wilson described this room in his conclusion.

"The professional folklorist sees folklore as something to be studied according to a systematic approach for the purpose of discovering some kind of knowledge relevant to it. The knowledge sought might concern its origin and dissemination, its structure, its bearing on ethnic history, or the light it sheds on the worldview or mental processes of the people to whom it belongs.

The amateur sees folklore as a source of aesthetic pleasure, a means of transportation to a simpler and pleasanter state of being, a striking expression of folk wisdom, or a bizarre instance of folk imagination. It is hardly possible to be both a professional and an amateur folklorist at one and the same moment, but we can be professionals at one time and amateurs at another. We can enjoy the ballad of 'Barbara Allen' and we can study it. It is very likely that those who choose to study do so because they first enjoyed. And retracing the historical course of a folktale does not spoil the pleasure we take in it. Knowledge may very well enhance enjoyment. It would be a pity if we were to become so professional that we should lose the amateur's attraction to folklore for its own sake. It would be a pity also if we were to suppose that folklore has no power to tell us anything about human beings and their group life.

"One of the great strengths of the Texas Folklore Society at the present time is that we are a mixture of amateurs and professionals and no one feels that he has to be one or the other exclusively. There is no conflict. We have profited by the best aspects of both attitudes. May we continue to do so in the future."

During his acceptance speech Wilson also had the pleasure of showing the first copies of James T. Bratcher's *Analytical Index to the Publications of the Texas Folklore Society, Volumes 1–36*. The *Index* was hot off the SMU Press and did not even have a dust jacket, but it was there. Wilson presented the first copy to Leroy Brown of Galveston, whose association with the Moody Foundation was instrumental in getting the Society $11,000 in grant money for its publication.

Wilson had inspired Jim Bratcher as a graduate student to undertake the making of an PTFS index for his Ph.D. dissertation, and Bratcher had taken his responsibilties to the limit by compiling not only a careful and complete index but had added two other sections. Part I is a specialized index consisting of tale types, motifs, and ballad numbers. Part II consists of a nine-part categorization of folktales with short summaries of each. And Part III is the alphabetical index.

Wilson wrote the foreword in which he states his and the TFS philosophy of collecting and preserving folklore from and for both amateur and professional folklorists. Wilson, who is ultimately responsible for the existence of this masterwork, concludes his foreword:

"The Society is like a man who has been making regular deposits in a savings account for more than half a century and at last discovers that he has grown rich little by little. Mr. Bratcher's index will reveal a kind of total which even long-time members of the Society are not aware of. To make it easier for students of folklore, and others as well, to find and use our materials is the goal of this index."

Jim Bratcher of the University of Texas at El Paso did a mind boggling amount of work on the Index, and he did it with complete academic professionalism. I doubt that the Society shall ever see its equal. Jim wrote the preface, and this editor wrote a brief history of the Society. Carl Hertzog, the Printer at the Pass was the layout and typographical advisor, and José Cisneros blessed the Society for the manyth time with the endsheet artwork.

Guynes Printing of El Paso printed one thousand books for $10,200. SMU Press did the dust jackets for $258.25 and distributed the book at $12.50 with 70% of the profit going to the Society (Maxwell to Abernethy, November 27, 1972). The dust jackets arrived after the book was in distribution, so we mailed dust jackets to all members in the July newsletter, hoping of course that they would buy a book to go with it. Members did not receive free *Indexes*.

Guynes had its production problems too; they mailed 190 copies of the *Index* with the endpapers upside down (Hartley to Abernethy, August 7, 1973).

This editor and Bratcher, who was a purist and classicist, argued briefly about including illustrations in the Index, but we did decide to saffron the predications with photographs and line drawings. The same philosophical sort of conflict arose over the dust jacket. In a March 25, 1973, letter Jim said, "(1) I prefer that the jacket not include any sort of biographical note or photo, and (2) not include quotations or prepared copy otherwise, excepting a list of TFS annuals." He added a post script that his name appear on the jacket without a "by" before it. "While I have not exactly 'authored' the book," he wrote, "I have done more than 'edit' or 'compile' it" (March 25, 1973). We all agreed on the latter, but felt the necessity to use the jacket space both artistically and practically, for TFS book promotion. When Margaret Hartley, the editor at SMU Press, asked for my input on the jacket, I replied, "I don't want the cover to look standard or be conservative or just traditional. I want men to frame the dust jacket to hang in their mistresses' apartments—and then leave the naked book on glass-topped coffee tables for its aphrodisiac effect" (March 28, 1973).

Wilson Hudson and this editor let out a high harmonic scream when we received our advanced copies and saw that the book had been copyrighted in Bratcher's name. One can find considerable correspondence between compiler and the secretary-editor on that point, considering that the Society had paid for publication.

Of all of the research that has been done since our beginning in 1909, and all the words written and books published, I do not know of anything that has more substance and stature than James T. Bratcher's *Analytical Index*.

Jim Bratcher got his doctorate, taught two years at UTEP, then went back to the farm. Bratcher is still writing and lives near San Antonio.

The book that was sent to members in 1973 was *Mody Boatright, Folklorist: A Collection of Essays* (ExB–15). The book was edited by Ernest B. Speck, Mody's son-in-law, of Sul Ross State University. Ernest had previously written the Mody Boatright biography for the Southwest Writers Series. Mody had served The University of Texas for over forty years, so it was fitting that Harry H. Ransom, Chancellor Emeritus and former TFS editor, write his autobiographical essay. And Mody's old friend, Wayland Hand of UCLA wrote the foreword. Wayland concluded his remarks by saying that Mody's work would stand "because it is innately honest, and because it avoids pretense in statement and is free of 'scholarly' manipulation" (ix).

After Mody's death in 1970 Wilson Hudson wrote the TFS officers and board (October 8, 1970) suggesting that memorial money be used for publishing a collection of Mody's essays. More money was raised and Frank Wardlaw and the University of Texas Press published the book for the Texas Folklore Society. UT Press paid for publication and marketed the book at $7.50. The Society bought for its members five hundred copies at forty-percent discount (Wardlaw to Abernethy, July 24, 1972).

When I say that *Mody Boatright, Folklorist* was the book sent to members in 1973, I should qualify that by saying that it was the second book sent to members. By mistake, UT Press mailed *John Breckinridge,* a book about a former Kentucky senator and vice president, to all TFS members the first time around. Then it mailed Mody Boatright. I cannot imagine that UT Press got all of its Breckinridge books back. If you are a longtime member of TFS and have a Breckinridge book in your bookcase, that is probably where you got it.

Our first-of-the-year balance $14,180.37 looked good in 1974 because we had the $11,000 Moody grant for Bratchers Index. That was the first time that the Society had accumulated a five-figure treasury. Unfortunately we had to pay that grand Moody sum to SMU Press. One member moved that we institute a registration fee to help pay for meetings and to improve the status of the TFS exchequer, but this was voted down overwhelmingly. Registration fees smacked of commercialism, of which the TFS would have no taint.

The Society was loaded with social and political liberals who were ready to soapbox for their various causes. This year we passed a resolution in support of the Big Thicket movement toward national park status. Before the applause had died, however, legal counselor Hermes Nye informed us that if we became involved in politics that we would lose our tax exempt status. We withdrew the resolution and returned to our folklore.

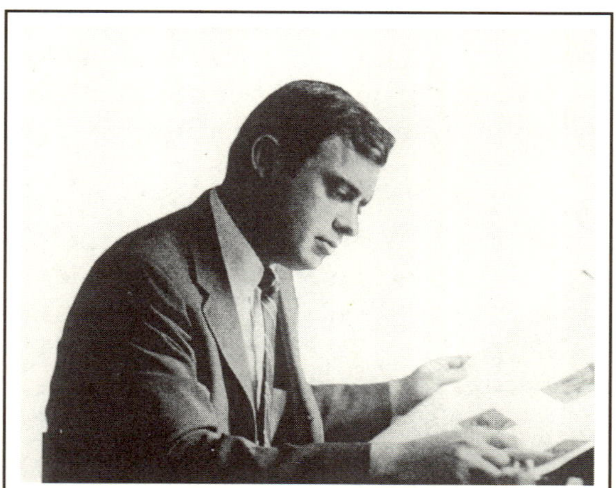

William D. Wittliff, publisher and founder of Encino Press, Austin

1974

Orlan L. Sawey (1920–1989)
President 1973–74 at Abilene
Chairman of departments of English at four different colleges, including Texas A&I at Kingsville, ordained minister of the Church of Christ, wrote the biography of Charles Siringo

Few will forget 1974 and the national embarrassment of Vice President Spiro Agnew's disbarment and "All the President's Men" being indicted as Watergate conspirators and President Richard Nixon himself resigning to prevent the trauma of impeachment. Nixon's vice president, Gerald Ford, was sworn in and to many citizens compounded the felonies by pardoning Nixon for any and all crimes he might have committed against the State. It was a politically ratty sort of year, relieved somewhat by Barbara Streisand singing "The Way We Were" and streakers running naked through the Academy Awards and during football games and on all the college campuses.

The Society had its fifty-eighth meeting at the Hilton Inn in Abilene, April 11–13. We were hosted that year by Mrs. L. E. Dudley and Miss McLauren Dudley of the General Federation of Women's Clubs, one of the few times a civic organization has been our host. But they were beautifully organized, produced mayors and other official greeters, and ran a tight ship for those three beautiful spring days.

The meeting was presided over by President Orlan Sawey (1920–1989) of Texas A&I University in Kingsville. Orlan had been a member since before the war, when he was a student at

A&I and working in the oil fields. He joined the army in June, 1941. Orlan went back to school after the war and did his doctorate under Mody Boatright at UT, with a dissertation on "The Cowboy Autobiography." Orlan retired as chairman of the English department at Texas A&I in 1977 and spent the rest of his life as a Church of Christ preacher.

Members were concerned about getting to Abilene that year. OPEC (Organization of Petroleum Exporting Countries) had instituted a fuel embargo and the U.S., as well as most of the fuel-using western world, was suffering from a fuel shortage. Filling stations were closed on Sundays, and the speed limit was reduced to fifty-five miles per hour, both measures to save on fuel. This crisis signaled the beginning of the end of the big-car company gas guzzlers and focused national attention on fuel saving. But most TFS members managed to make the long drive to Abilene anyhow, and we had a full meeting.

The meeting papers included signs of the times with topics on bumper stickers, which were a new means of communication at that time; underground newspapers, with which the young confronted "the establishment"; and the folklore of marijuana, which was the drug of choice. The banquet speech was given by Robert Flynn and was his first presentation on the Baptists of Chillicothe, a topic which he has often used and refined over the years. Waco Baptist Martha Emmons was not amused, but most of his audience were—and still are.

The Society decided that year to define the duties of the various officers, particularly at meeting time. As included in the minutes of the 1974 meeting, the duties were:

"1) The president has the honor of being president and acting as nominal coordinator. He is in charge of the banquet Friday night, works with the vice president and the secretary-editor in choosing the speaker, and is the master of ceremonies. He also presides at the business meeting, appoints committees, and sees that all necessary resolutions are written and presented.

2) The vice president is the program chairman. He selects the section chairmen and the papers to be presented and arranges the order of their presentation. By vote the Society decided against the presentation of absentee papers, and by custom the program chairman does not present a paper.

3) The chairman of local arrangements is in charge of all local arrangements. He is usually the one who extends the invitation and helps finance the meeting. Sometimes the host is also elected to be vice president. This sounds very practical but it results in an overload of work on the host/vice president.

4) The secretary mails the announcement and the rough-draft program and sees to the printing of the final program.

By agreement and in cooperation these duties are frequently exchanged and re-arranged."

The Society went into 1974 with the precarious balance of $2,158.32. We had between four and five hundred members, so the expected dues would add $3500 more, plus royalties. The average price of a PTFS was between $5000 and $6000, with the cost rising annually, so we stayed in business by the skin of our teeth.

The publication for 1974 was *The Folklore of Texan Cultures* (PTFS 38), the Society's contribution to The American Bicentennial celebration. Bill Wittliff and Encino Press published the book, and because it was so large Bill wanted to do it in two volumes. In the end we put *Texan Cultures* in one large volume and bound 3512 books for $11,655.62. This was a large expense for a Society, whose annual income from dues and royalties was about a third of that price. We escaped bankruptcy through grants received from several foundations: Temple of Diboll, Hamman of Houston, Pollock of Dallas, Kempner of Galveston, and Tellepsen of Houston.

I had envisioned a folklore of Texan cultures book from my editorial beginning. I had worked with the Institute of Texan Cultures since its opening in 1968 and had been one of the founders of the Texas Folklife Festival in 1972. So nothing was more logical than a book celebrating this state's ethnic diversity, as the ITC had so done. *Texan Cultures* was a labor of love but it was also a labor, because I had to find writers to cover the two dozen different Texan cultures—Danes, Slavonians, Japanese, et al. As I look back over the correspondence generated by that publication, I am reminded of all the interesting people who were a part of it. Jim Snyder of SFA's art department did the endsheets based on Terry Jordan's Texas ethnic map, and Dan Beaty of SFA's music department scored the necessary music. The book was shipped to members in December, and became our fastest selling publication, going out of print in two years.

The Folklore of Texan Cultures is just one of a flurry of celebrations of ethnicity in the U. S. in the past generation. As interesting as this study was, I frequently wonder whether we overemphasize our nationalities and whether some get so carried away with their own ethnicity that they forget that in the big picture we are one people, state, nation in which ethnicity should get lost in humanity.

But, "Glory be to God for dappled things . . . . "

And for streakers!

Academicians have a hard time drawing the thin line between popular culture and folklore. I consider pop culture to be more transient than folklore, quicker to come and to go—like mood rings and pet rocks and streaking.

That was the year, 1974, that I was looking out the window as I lectured on Hamlet, and here came a buck nekkid guy in tennis shoes and a baseball cap, streaking past our building. Every student in class made it to the window in time for a peek. On another occasion, a fellow at SFA was given a ticket for riding naked through the campus on his motorcycle; he was not wearing a helmet. In desperation, Dr. Ralph Steen, then president of SFA, blocked off the dormitory road and "countenanced" a one-last streaking and beer party within those limits. Male and female students streaked in couples, singly, in groups, danced the can-can on a dormitory roof, and went generally wild for six hours. As a folklorist I reluctantly went, as an academic duty, of course. And I certainly saw another layer of some of my students.

Betty Boatright's paisano

1975

Ernest B. Speck (1917–1995)
President 1974–75 at Houston
Professor of English at Sul Ross State University, Mody Boatright's son-in-law and editor of *Mody Boatright, Folklorist,* worked in Paris for the International News Service, authority on rural customs and practices

Nobody really expected the North Vietnamese to honor the cease-fire agreement. We had just wanted out! So, it was no surprise when the North Vietnamese started overrunning the outskirts of Saigon, and the remaining Americans and their allies had twenty-four hours to get out of town. The picture of the panic as the last helicopters left the American embassy compound is one that will haunt our generation forever. At about the same time the Khmer Rouge took over Cambodia, and the killing fields were being tilled for the bloody planting that followed. This was a bad year for Indochina.

But it was a good year back home. I am forever reminded that even as the world goes to hell in a handbasket, every individual must work at his own job. In 1942 and '43, Mody Boatright kept the Society going and counseled members that the Texas Folklore Society must not be a casualty of the war. In the late Sixties and early Seventies the TFS maintained its equilibrium in the midst of national social insanities.

The January newsletter and meeting invitation contained the editor's main concern of publications. *The Folklore of Texan Cultures* (PTFS 38–1974) was in the members' hands, and the manuscript for *Some Still Do* (PTFS 39–1975) was ready to ship to Bill

Wittliff and Encino Press. *Some Still Do* opened with Wilson Hudson's Fellowship speech, "Amateur and Professional Folklorists," and contained essays on Texas customs, past and present.

Some Still Do was another fun book to do. I had spent several days photographing the cowboys at the Waggoner Ranch, where my grandad had worked back in the 1880s and '90s, so I wrote about cowboy customs. We had articles on making syrup and buttermilk, mud-daub chimneys, and where to find the proper clay to eat. Wittliff cut it close and mailed the book in December of 1975. Bill Wittliff knew how to blend the best of paper and print, and he and Encino never did a book that the Society was not proud of. Bill did for our generation of editors what Carl Hertzog did for Frank Dobie; he made us look better than we were.

I was sending out my never-ending call for new writers and fresh manuscripts. I had sent out a call in 1972 for a family saga annual but, surprising to me, got little response. I pursued that topic for twenty-five years without profit. Several of us were talking then about using as the TFS annual an LP record album of Brownie McNeil's "Jalisco," John Q. Anderson's "Waco Girl," Jo Lyday's "Razorback Hog," Américo Paredes' "Rancho Grande," Martha Emmons' "The Adulteration of Ole King David," Hermes Nye, Roger Abrahams, Lu Mitchell, and a bunch of others. I regret now that the Society missed that opportunity to tape and preserve those performing folklorists. But as always, the problem was money. Also, as early as 1975 the editor was planning a history of the TFS and was soliciting reminiscences from members.

For the first time in a long time, the Society, with the cooperation of SMU Press and Encino Press, had every one of its books in print, back to Stith Thompson's PTFS 1–1916. The Society offered a package deal of thirty-eight books plus Bratcher's Index for $200.67, or $5.15 per book. Sales were fair.

Royalties from all TFS publications for 1975 were $6,135.68, for all books. We also had acquired some grant money for publication of *Folklore of Texan Cultures*, so we closed the books for the year with a healthy balance of $13,009.30.

We met at the Marriott in Houston that beautiful spring, hosted by Anne R. Phillips and the University of Houston. Memorable moments among many on that years program were Jim Lee's paper in which he introduced the membership to the female category concept of "mothers and others"; and Guy Logsdon, impeccably westernly attired, delivering a paper on western swing to the admiring sighs of the women present; and Stanley Marcus telling tales told about Nieman-Marcus; and the meeting room hanging with fabric folk designs from Guatemala, brought in by Geoffrey Grimes.

Ernest Speck (1917–1995), Professor of English at Sul Ross State University at Alpine, was president that year. Ernest was an authority on rural customs and practices, and he was one of the few men I know who opened pecans with a pocket knife.

Margaret Hartley wrote (March 13, 1975) that SMU Press had received a five thousand dollar Texas Commission on the Arts grant to publish a second, revised edition of William A. Owens' *Texas Folk Songs* (PTFS 23–1950). The grant money was about half of what the press needed to get the book on the stands, so the Society did help minimally.

We lost a rash of long-time members between 1974 and 1975: John Q. Anderson (1916–1975), J. Mason Brewer (1896–1975), Bertha McKee Dobie (1890–1974), Mabel Major (1894–1974), John A. Lomax, Jr. (1907–1974) and Margaret Marable Lomax (1908–1973).

If you still do not remember 1975, as a folklorist do you remember mood rings and pet rocks? These were some of our pop culture/folklore items for the year. Or perhaps both items were outrageous scams foisted on a gullible public. Mood rings contained heat-sensitive quartz crystals which changed color as the wearer changed moods from happy to sad to mad. If the wearer wanted to know how he felt, all he had to do was look at his ring. Pet rocks were sold in small boxes with air holes and instructions for their care and feeding. People bought pet rocks to the tune of making their creator a millionaire.

1976

Joyce Gibson Roach
President 1975–76 at Arlington
English Department, Texas Christian University, 1984–1997, teacher, lecturer, author, journalist, three-time Spur Award winner from Western Writers of America, member Texas Institute of Letters, Fellow of Texas State Historical Association and of Clements Center at SMU

I will begin this year's entry with a jaundiced editorial passage from the February 16, 1976, newsletter:

"I hope this Bicentennial year finds you firm of purpose and strong in the faith. You'll have to be both to get through all the hoopla of '76."

Five months later in the July 5, 1976, minutes of the Arlington meeting the editor had changed his tune completely and concluded:

"I shed some of my cynicism yesterday [Fourth of July]. Like most of you, I had committeed, pageanted, and paraded until I had about Bicentennialed out, and I was ready to see the Glorious Fourth over with. But the day wasn't like that at all. We had a good watermelon, it didn't rain, and as I watched some of the CBS coverage I really did feel what we were supposed to feel—the beauty of this country and the kinship of its people and the pride of belonging to it and it to me. And I got to top the day off in the best of ways. A couple of SFA students (kicker-hippie blends) got married on a green mountain top overlooking the Atascosa Creek bottoms, and the East Texas String Ensemble played for the occasion. It was a grand way to celebrate 200 years-plus of rich living. We played "Black Mountain Rag" and people danced on the hillside and drank beer and ate barbecue and watched the sun go down—and it was all so fine and symbolic that I got choked up every time I let myself think about it. So I bought it all, all the hoopla and the tall ships and fireworks and guns firing. I look back on the day with all 50 stars in my sky-blue eyes, and if it would accomplish anything I'd paint myself with red and white stripes and run up a flag pole."

North and South Vietnam united, which was what they were trying to do all along, and Jimmy Carter was elected as president, which proved that Yellow Dog Democrats were still flourishing.

Joyce Roach of Keller, Texas, presided over the sixtieth Bicentennial celebration meeting at the Ramada Inn in Arlington on April 15–17, 1976. Joyce was (still is) a school teacher and business woman. She was a cowgirl and a writer, and she put the two talents together in her book *The Cowgirls* and won the Spur Award for western writing.

The economy that year dictated motel prices at $22.50 for a double and $6.25 for the banquet ticket. Treasurer Edwin Gaston reported a balance at the end of 1975 of $13,009.30, which was an improvement over the previous year, but not much considering that the Encino Press bill for *What's Going On* was $9,357.87 for 2500 copies. The Society was getting steady in the saddle financially, but as our income increased so did our living and publication expenses.

Among interesting papers dealing with "old" and "new" folklore was a panel on veterinarian Ben K. Green, whose horse trader books were Alfred A. Knopf best sellers at the time. Ben Green had published eleven books between 1967 and his death in 1974 and had received awards from western writers, Cowboy Hall of Fame, and the Texas Institute of Letters. The only problem with his books, the panel concluded, was to decide where truth stopped and story telling began. And this included Ben's life as well as his tales. I read with pleasure several of his books and concluded that he would have had to have lived at least three lives to have had as many experiences as he wrote about. Ben Green's life and literature are still matters of controversy.

The Thursday night hootenanny went into the wee morning hours, with Ramada Inn people coming in periodically asking us to leave so they could clean up. The Ramada, fearful of Bob

Bullock's boys snooping for violations of liquor licenses, issued the order of "no beer at the hoot." Ernestine Sewell, chairwoman of local arragements, saw to it that husband Charles Linck solved the refreshment problem by bringing in several cases of beer and icing them down in Elmer Kelton's bathtub. Thereafter, Charles and Ernestine's son Buzz patrolled the halls as hooters spliced the mainbrace with goods from Elmer's bathtub. Meanwhile Bill Brett provided extra sustenance for himself and others with a quart fruit jar of pine-top white lightning (Sewell to editor, March 1, 1991).

What's Going On (In Modern Texas Folklore) (PTFS 40–1976) was the Society's response to Leland Sonnichsen's banquet address, "The Poor Wayfaring Scholar," which he gave at the 1975 meeting in Houston. Sonnichsen had accused folklorists of ignoring the modern folklore, the poplore and popular culture that was circulating all around them. Members cornered Leland after the banquet and pointed out that the Society over the past several years had published as much modern as old-time folklore. *What's Going On* contained poplore about cobras at K-Mart, Nieman-Marcus, Jack Ruby, smoking pot, and redneck rock, among others. Doing research for their papers, Joe Lomax had his film confiscated at a zydeco barrel house, and Robert Russell was suspected of being the fuzz while he was researching a marijuana smoke-out. The Society was trying to stay au courant.

What's Going On concluded with seven articles on music of the Seventies—gospel, redneck rock, C&W, among others. Stan Alexander concluded the volume with an article on Backwoods Beer Busts, a Seventies Woodstock phenomenon that the East Texas String Ensemble was regularly involved in. The generation gap between us (the Strings) and them (the hippies) was still narrow enough that we could step across. Those gigs were certainly educational!

1977

William H. Hardin

President 1976–1977 at El Paso

Retired army, worked for the United States Postal Service

The Society met at the Paso del Norte Hotel in El Paso in 1977. For the third time in our history we met in conjunction with our neighbors in New Mexico. In 1938 Leland Sonnichsen invited us to El Paso to meet with the Hispanic Institute of New Mexico. In 1952 President Haldeen Braddy arranged a joint meeting with the New Mexico Folklore Society. In 1977 James M. Day and John O. West arranged the meeting in El Paso, which many members felt was half way across the known world. It is the only meeting I know about for which a bus was chartered to make the journey. The total charter for the Arrow Coach Lines bus out of Brownwood was $1,025.00. That was divided by the number of persons on board. Members filled the bus, and most of the riders enjoyed the camaraderie for the nine-hour trip.

We did everything in pairs that year, being very careful of the feelings of our sister state. William H. Hardin (–1989) of Houston (retired army with two beautiful daughters), the TFS president, and Muriel Latham-Pfeifer, president of the New Mexico Folklore Society, shared presiding duties. The program chairwomen very agreeably split the sessions down the middle. We had a lot of papers that year!

The Printer at the Pass Carl Hertzog attended, as did the Society's own favorite artist, El Paso's José Cisneros. Geoffrey Grimes, President of the Texas Cultural Alliance, mounted an exhibit of children's art from all over the world. For Friday evening we had a mariachi band for the cocktail hour, a dance demonstration at the banquet, and a late night field trip across the Rio Grande to visit cantinas in Juarez. That was a rich and memorable meeting.

The book for 1977 was Howard N. Martin's *Myths & Folktales of the Alabama-Coushatta Indians of Texas* (ExB–16). Bill Wittliff's Encino Press was the publisher and Barbara Whitehead did the woodcut illustrations. Howard, who in 1977 was the Director of Research of Houston's Chamber of Commerce, was reared in Polk County, grew up with some of the Indians on the reservation, and seriously collected Alabama-Coushatta folklore from 1930 through 1940. At the University of Texas Howard studied under Eugene Barker and Frank Dobie. Dobie urged him to get his stories in print, and he did so in 1946 with a seminal collection in pamphlet form and in the Society's PTFS 21, *Mexican Border Ballads and Other Lore*. This 1977 publication of Alabama and Coushatta tales was the result of Howard's life-long interest in the Indians of Polk County and is the definitive collection of their folktales. The Society bought the book from Encino Press, rather than paying for publication. We saved about three thousand dollars by using this extra book.

The Society's publishing problem in 1977 was that *The Folklore of Texan Cultures* was out of print, and to get the Society's best seller back in print would cost over $6000. That was close to the amount which we had on hand—$5,964,81 as of January 1, 1977—to pay for next year's 1978 miscellany, *Paisanos*. During that same time, I was working on 1979's *Built in Texas*, which I knew was going to cost a bundle to publish. But, this sort of financial problem was nothing new to the Society, and we eventually got all of the books to TFS members, and we survived.

That was the year that the Texas Folklore Society, the Institute of Texan Cultures, the Center for Intercultural Studies in Folklore and Ethnomusicology at the University of Texas, and the American Folklife Center sponsored the Conference on Texas Culture: Preservation and Presentation on September 30 to October l, 1977, at the Institute of Texan Cultures in San Antonio. The purpose of the conference was "to provide the opportunity for folklorists, representatives of state and federal agencies, and others engaged in activities related to folk culture to discuss efforts which preserve and present our folk cultural heritage." We spoke many words with much sound and fury "but evermore came out by the same door wherein [we] went." I alienated some members of the audience with my own folkloric philosophizing, and some of them alienated me.

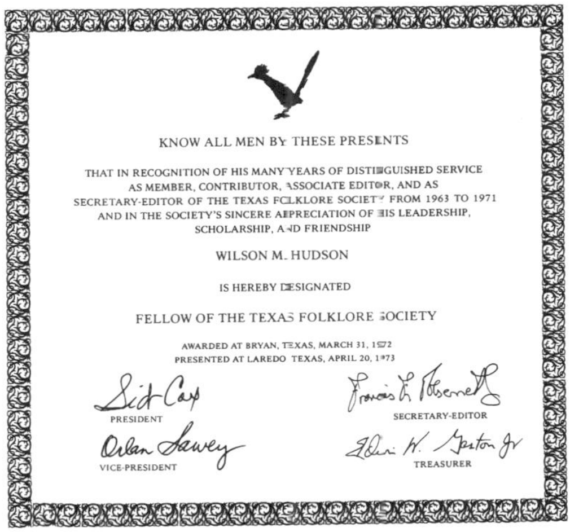
KNOW ALL MEN BY THESE PRESENTS

THAT IN RECOGNITION OF HIS MANY YEARS OF DISTINGUISHED SERVICE AS MEMBER, CONTRIBUTOR, ASSOCIATE EDITOR, AND AS SECRETARY-EDITOR OF THE TEXAS FOLKLORE SOCIETY FROM 1963 TO 1971 AND IN THE SOCIETY'S SINCERE APPRECIATION OF HIS LEADERSHIP, SCHOLARSHIP, AND FRIENDSHIP

WILSON M. HUDSON

IS HEREBY DESIGNATED

FELLOW OF THE TEXAS FOLKLORE SOCIETY

AWARDED AT BRYAN, TEXAS, MARCH 31, 1972
PRESENTED AT LAREDO TEXAS, APRIL 20, 1973

PRESIDENT | SECRETARY-EDITOR

VICE-PRESIDENT | TREASURER

Wilson M. Hudson, Fellow of the Texas Folklore Society, with wife Gertrude and Elizabeth Nye

1978

Ernestine Sewell Linck
President 1977–78 at Nacogdoches
Professor of English at the University of Texas at Arlington, student of and model for Native American art; co-author of *Eats: A Folk History of Texas Food,* 1989 winner of Texas Institute of Letters award; now lives in Commerce

In 1978 we knew that we were in runaway inflation as prices of goods rose dramatically and wages rose slowly, if at all. The Yankee dollar, that was at most times the world's measure of value, was dropping rapidly as the Japanese yen and European currency rose. The Senate ratified the treaty to give the Canal to Panama in 1999. The Equal Rights Amendment to the Constitution was still hustling state votes. And if you need a real horror to mark 1978, that was the year that over nine hundred of the Peoples' Temple in Jonestown, Guyana, drank cyanide cocktails at the behest of their loving pastor, the Reverend Jim Jones.

Ernestine Sewell reported on that year:

"In Nacogdoches, 1978, it was my time to be president. [Husband] Charles [Linck] and I gave an autograph party before the Thursday hoot. Paul Patterson's *Crazy Women in the Rafters,* Bill Brett's *Stolen Steers,* and Joyce Roach's *Cowgirls,* and the 1978 PTFS *Paisanos* were our featured books. We also arranged for David L. Middleton from San Antonio to show his film, 'The Newton Boys: Portrait of an Outlaw Gang.' It gets funnier every time one sees it. The Friday night banquet gave me a chance to show off. I had a dress made of Guatemalan cloth *shot with gold,* I'll have you know. I wore about six turquoise necklaces, that many bracelets on each arm, rings on every finger. (I have to dress this way to keep ahead of Charles and his colorful coats. The only person to best him was Von-Maszewski who showed up at a banquet one time wearing a bright, bright coat with electric lights flashing.) One of the better things I did, I think, was to pass over an invocation and have Jim Harris read a poem he had written to his new son Hawk (Sewell to editor March 4, 1991)."

The Texas Folklore Society met at the Fredonia Inn in Nacogdoches, March 23–25, 1978. Ernestine Sewell, who was a professor of English at the University of Texas at Arlington—as well as a prolific author, weaver of fine wools, artist in Indian jewelry, and printer at Cow Hill Press—presided that year. We had planned to make this meeting a joint Texas-Louisiana meeting, since we were so close to the Sabine, but were not able to match their meeting time.

The most significant business of the 1978 meeting was the raising of dues to ten dollars for individuals and fifteen for families. Publication prices were increasing annually. Perhaps the most memorable incident—that is, we are still talking about it—was a forty-five! minute paper by one of the Society's grande dames with chairman Glen Lich sitting alongside, mouth open, unable to staunch the flow.

Willie Earl Tindall of San Augustine put on the Thursday night beer and barbecue. The East Texas String Ensemble, then in their prime, played afterward, doing away with the usual members' hootenanny, which we had after the banquet on Friday night.

Paisanos: A Folklore Miscellany (PTFS 41–1978) was sent out of Encino Press early enough for distribution at the meeting. Bill Wittliff always did beautiful book designs, but this is my favorite of the books he did for the Society. Linda Miller Roach, a professional wildlife artist and photographer from Nacogdoches, drew a dozen paisanos for illustrations, and these are still the best roadrunner pictures I have found.

The paisano, or roadrunner, had been the Society's emblem since H. B. Parks sponsored it in 1932 and Ben Carlton Mead drew a stylized roadrunner for the title page of *Tone the Bell Easy* (PTFS 10–1932). In 1937 Betty Boatright drew a paisano for the Society, and Frank Dobie took it over for his own—and I took it over for our letterhead and am still using it. It was mandatory that I begin *Paisanos* with Frank Dobie's "The Paisano's Cactus Corral" (from *Texas Folk and Folklore*, PTFS 26, 289–295) and José Cisneros' drawing which went with it. There were many more paisano illustrations during the Society's history, and Society members refer to each other as "paisanos," or fellow countrymen-Texans: thus the title.

As a result of frequent requests from folklore researchers and writers, the Society commissioned Willie Earl Tindall and Lee Sullenger, both from SFA's Ralph Steen Library, to compile a list of publishers of articles on Texas folklore to include in *Paisanos*. Their "Publishers of Texas Folklore" became a standard reference work.

Encino ran 2,500 copies of *Paisanos* and bound 1,500. This production, along with shipping costs, cost the Society $8,450. Our balance at the beginning of 1978 was $14,136.85, so we were able to pay for *Paisanos* and still have some money for planning and operation.

In spite of which seeming affluence, all was not happy in the publishing business. Bill and I, although we remained friends, were never in agreement about the financial arrangement that I inherited when I became editor. I quote from a letter I wrote Bill on January 17, 1973, soon after receiving the bill for *Observations and Reflections*, the PTFS for 1972. I opened with a paragraph which questioned why the final price was more than the original estimate. I continued:

"Question #2: You boggled my mind with this sentence: 'I assume we are to bill the TFS on the copies we sent for you at 40% of the $7.50 dues.' I pause to un-boggle. The 1972 dues were $5.00. We don't get $7.50 per member until the 1973 dues start coming in, and they are supposed to cover the Boatright anthology. *And surely you don't mean that we are to be billed again for the members' books in addition to production costs. After we pay for the production of the books they should be ours* [Editor's italics. This was our basic dispute.] . . . Write me a letter explaining our financial arrangements, agreements, percentages, and that sort of thing. I shall study it."

In 1973 Bill believed the Society should go up on its dues to ten dollars per member to pay for publications. I wanted to hold the dues at $7.50. Bill was right; we did need to increase our dues. This conflict lasted throughout the Society's association with Encino. In 1977 I wanted Bill to print another edition of *Folklore of Texan Cultures* at his expense, because it was a good seller and had gone out of print the year before. He expected that the Society should pay for it, and we battled over that. Looking back, I think that he was right on that point also. But I was right about the inequities in double payment for books, i.e., paying for the publication and then buying them for the members. So, by 1979 I was looking for another publisher, in spite of my knowing that Bill Wittliff was the best book designer in these parts and that Encino was the classiest press. Bill and I parted friendly but agreeing that it was time to part.

One of the reasons that I was willing to cut the ties with Encino was that Frank Wardlaw, longtime director of the University of Texas Press, had moved to A&M Press and had told me that he was interested in doing the TFS publications. He had seen the illustrations, prefatory material, and some of the articles for *Built in Texas* and was impressed with its beginnings. You can imagine my consternation when I learned that Frank had resigned at A&M because of health and had gone back to North Carolina. Lloyd Lyman assumed the directorship in the summer of 1978, and I sent the illustrations and an incomplete manuscript for *Built in Texas* to him. Lloyd turned it over to his board, and the reader gave it a weak report on the grounds that the essays were uneven in quality. That has always been a characteristic of TFS publications, constructed as they are.

I guess that one of the lowest points in my editing career—in my life, really!—was the October night that I met Lloyd Lyman at a parking lot in Bryan and he returned to me the manuscript for *Built in Texas*. I went on to Austin and talked to Wittliff. He said that he would do the book, but he was no happier about doing it than I was about his doing it.

And then the Lord smiled upon me and a good woman came to my rescue, as has so often happened in my life.

Frances Brannen Vick of Waco and her brother Joe Pat Brannen had recently fallen heir to a herd of Piney Woods cattle. Their brand was a heart with an E in the middle. Fran and Joe Pat were the E-Heart Land and Cattle Company. They sold some of the cattle that fall, and Fran took her part and started a publishing company, the E-Heart Press. She needed a first book to publish, so she called me to see if I knew about one. Did I ever!

We met on a bitter-cold November night at the Red Lantern Cafe in Buffalo, half way between her Waco and my Nacogdoches, and struck a bargain between E-Heart Press and the Texas Folklore Society. The Society would pay the cost of publication and the Press would produce and distribute the book for a forty-sixty split, the sixty to the Press.

This is the way Fran told the story of the financial part of that adventure in a June 3, 1998, letter to the editor: "Ross and I had a banker friend in Waco—remember, Ross was a banker at one point in his checkered career—so I went to Bill for a loan to start E-Heart Press. As a friend, he was concerned about my losing money, but since he knew that I would repay him, he gave me the loan. He later told Ross—after I had repaid the loan—that he had been elated to make that loan because when the bank examiners came in and wanted to know about women and minority loans he would have one to show them! This was in 1978, the years before women had achieved much equality in such matters as loans."

Fran was new at the publishing business and her first book cost her the rest of her herd, but in 1979 she published *Built in Texas* (PTFS 42), which, as far as I am concerned, is the best book to come out of my editorship and time in the Texas Folklore Society.

Edwin W. Gaston, Treasurer from 1971 to 1996

Meetings and Publications of the Texas Folklore Society 1971 to 1978

Fifty-fifth annual meeting, San Antonio, April 9–10, 1971, held at the Menger Hotel, hosted by San Antonio College

Officers

President: Ralph Houston, Southwest Texas State University

Vice-President: Bessie Pearce, San Antonio College

Treasurer: Arthur M. Cory, The University of Texas, Austin

Secretary and Editor: Wilson M. Hudson, The University of Texas, Austin

Councilors: Sidney Cox, Texas A&M; James M. Day, UTEP; Conrad Dunagan, Monahans; Martha Emmons, Baylor: Anne Phillips, University of Houston

Directors: Wilson M. Hudson, The University of Texas, James W. Lee, North Texas State; Hermes Nye, Dallas; John O. West, UTEP; E. Hudson Long, Baylor

Paisano Advisory Board: John Q. Anderson University of Houston; Edwin W. Gaston, Jr., Stephen F. Austin State University; Norman L. McNeil, Sul Ross State

Program

Friday morning session:

Chairman: Hermes Nye, Dallas

"The Echo Man: Chronicler of Wild Men in a Wild Land, 1875–77," Ernestine P. Sewell, U.T. at Arlington

"Edgar Rye, Townbuilder of North Central Texas," Charles E. Linck, Jr., East Texas State

Folktales: Thomas Hardy, Florence and Wessex," Grace Pleasant Wellborn, Texas Tech

"How Firm a Foundation," Imogene B. Dickey, North Texas State

"Handwriting on the Wall," Francis E. Abernethy, Stephen F. Austin State

"Lawlessness in Texas Boom Areas," James L. Evans, Pan American College

Friday afternoon session:

Chairman: Martha Emmons, Baylor

"Mody Boatright: The Genesis of a Folklorist," Ernest B. Speck, Sul Ross State

"The Impact of the Railroad on American Folk Song," Ann Carpenter, Angelo State University

"The Headless Boots," Jerre A. Dulock, Tarrant County Junior College

"Hallelujah Thine the Glory," Joyce Roach, Keller

"Peele's Old Wives' Tale and Tale-Type 425A, " James Bratcher, UTEP

"Guardians, Surviving Folkways," John Igo, San Antonio College

Dinner toastmaster: Ralph Houston, President

Speaker: Francis L. Utley, Ohio State University, "Folk Jests About Heaven and Hell"

Saturday session:

Chairman: John O. West, UTEP

"There Were Once Two Ethiopians, Sambo and Rastus," James W. Byrd, East Texas State

"Paving the Streets with Flowers: Corpus Christi Day in Sitges, Spain," Charles B. Martin, North Texas State University

"Shotgun Shacks of the Texas Panhandle," Sylvia Grider, Pampa
"The Old Order Changeth," Stuart Pearce, San Antonio
"From Alfalfa to Zea Mays: Traditional Aids for Beauty and Good Grooming," Peggy Skaggs, Angelo State University
Business meeting

Diamond Bessie & The Shepherds. PTFS XXXVI. Wilson M. Hudson, ed. Austin, The Encino Press, 1971.

CONTENTS

Fifty-sixth annual meeting, College Station, March 30–April 1, 1972, held at Ramada Inn, hosted by Texas A&M University

Officers
President: Bessie M. Pearce, San Antonio College
Vice-President: Sid Cox, Texas A&M
Treasurer: Edwin W. Gaston, Jr., Stephen F. Austin State University
Secretary-Editor: Francis Edward Abernethy, Stephen F. Austin State University
Councilors: Ralph Houston, Southwest Texas State University; James M. Day, UTEP; Conrad Dunagan, Monahans; Martha Emmons, Baylor; Anne Phillips, University of Houston
Directors: Hermes Nye (1972), Dallas; John O. West (1972), UTEP; E. Hudson Long (1973), Baylor; James W. Lee (1974), North Texas State; Wilson M. Hudson (1974), The University of Texas
Paisano Advisory Board: John Q. Anderson, University of Houston; Edwin W. Gaston, Jr., Stephen F. Austin State University; Norman L. McNeil, Sul Ross State University
Program Chairman: Sid Cox, Texas A&M

Program
Friday morning session:
Chairman: Peggy Skaggs, Angelo State
"She Is Mounted and Gone," Joyce Roach, Keller
"A Day in the Life of Maria da Silva, Cabrocha of Rio's Hillsides," Susan Mellor, Bryan
"Ticks on the Catfish: West Texas Drouth in Folklore," Ann Carpenter, Angelo State
"William B. Travis: Legend and Fact," Archie P. McDonald, Stephen F. Austin State
"Mattias Splitlog, Indian Builder," E.L. Harrington, Texas A&M
"Snipe Huntin' and Hog Killin': The Initiation of Theron Hunnicut," Donald W. Hatley, Northwestern State College of Louisiana
"Buttermilk is Beautiful," Ernest B. Speck, Sul Ross State University
Friday afternoon session:
Chairman: Martha Emmons, Baylor
"Grass," Mrs. J. Frank Dobie, Austin
"Texas Prairies as the Pioneer Saw Them," Brown Collins, Stanton
"A Honey of a Remedy," Charles Dromgocle, Sour Lake
"Renaissance Lore and Woman's Lib," Jeri Tanner, Texas Tech
"Six Hens and a Man Fowl," Annie Randle, Waco
"Folk Poetry: From Darkey to Negro to Black," James W. Byrd, East Texas State University, and Don Watson, Tyler
"Tequila in Fact and Folklore," James L. Evans, Pan American College
Recreational period: Directors: H.S. Creswell and Henry L. Alsmeyer, Jr.
Dinner Toastmaster: Bessie Pearce, President
Speaker: J. Mason Brewer, East Texas State University, "I Knew Them All"
Saturday session:
Chairman: Warren Walker, Texas Tech
"Poor Boy Menus and Receipts for Hard Times in Texas," Orlan L. Sawey, Texas A&I
"Indexing the TFS Publications," James T. Bratcher, UTEP
"Tailholt CSD," Sid Cox, Texas A&M
"Made in U.S.A.: An American Contribution to Art," Ina McQuaid, Garland
"The Automobile in Folklore," Roy L. Swift, Floresville
"From Amnesia to Illegitimacy: the Soap Opera as Contemporary Folklore," Sarah Greene, Gilmer
"Of a Will and a Wind," Jean Dugat, Beeville
Business Meeting

Observations and Reflections on Texas Folklore. PTFS XXXVII. Francis Edward Abernethy, ed. Austin: The Encino Press, 1972.

CONTENTS

Fifty-seventh annual meeting, Laredo, April 19–21, 1973, held at La Posada Inn, hosted by Texas A&I in Kingsville, Texas A&I at Laredo, and Laredo Junior College.

Officers

President: Sid Cox, Texas A&M University

Vice-President: Orlan Sawey, Texas A&I University in Kingsville

Treasurer: Edwin W. Gaston, Jr., Stephen F. Austin State University

Secretary-Editor: Francis E. Abernethy, Stephen F. Austin State University

Councilors: James M. Day, Conrad Dunagan, Martha Emmons, Anne Phillips, Mary Elizabeth Nye, Bessie M. Pearce

Directors: E. Hudson Long, Baylor University; James W. Lee, North Texas State; Wilson M. Hudson, The University of Texas; John O. West, The University of Texas at El Paso; Francis E. Abernethy, Stephen F. Austin State

Paisano Advisory Board: John Q. Anderson, University of Houston; Edwin W. Gaston, Jr., Stephen F. Austin State; Norman L. McNeil, Sul Ross State

Program Chairman: Orlan Sawey, Texas A&I University in Kingsville

Program

Friday morning session:

Chairman: Joyce Gibson Roach, Keller

"Laredo," Allen Briggs, Texas A&I University at Laredo

"Horse Handles and How Come They're Called That," Paul Patterson, Sierra Blanca

"J.M. Shannon, Folk Hero of the Sheep Industry," Ann Carpenter, Angelo State

"From Mesquite and Cactus to Limequats and Star Ruby Grapefruit," James L. Evans, Pan American University

"Some Baptists are Primitive," Martin Shockley, North Texas State University

"I Remember Chautauqua," Marjorie Shockley, North Texas State University

"Corn—The Stalk of Life," Ernest Speck, Sul Ross State

Friday afternoon: Chairman: Hermes Nye, Dallas;
"Juan Diego Crosses the Rio Grande," John O. West, UTEP
"The Development of Chicano Music in Texas," Jose Reyna, Texas A&I in Kingsville
"The Agringado Jest in Texas-Mexican Culture," Jose E. Limon, The University of Texas
"Tradition as a Positive Force in the Lives of Candelilla Wax Makers," Joe Graham, Sul Ross State University
Dinner Toastmaster: Sidney Cox, President
Presentation of Wilson M. Hudson as Fellow of the Texas Folklore Society
Response: Wilson M. Hudson, The University of Texas, "Amateur and Professional Folklorists"
Saturday session:
Chairman: Joseph M. Doggett, University of Houston
"How about Another Helpin', Please?," Jerre A. Dulock, South Campus, Tarrant County Junior College
"Traveling Anecdotes in Black and White," James W. Byrd, East Texas State
"You Buy Rug?," Ernestine Sewell and Charles E. Linck, The University of Texas at Arlington
"Geophagy in This Generation," Ava Bush, Stephen F. Austin State University
"Chain Letters: A Twentiety-Century Folk Practice," Robert J. Duncan, Mesquite
"The Cowboy Ballad as Parody," Orlan Sawey, Texas A&I University

Fifty-eighth annual meeting, Abilene, April 11, 12, and 13, 1974 held at the Hilton Inn, at the invitation of Mrs. L.E. Dudley, member in good standing and spirit.
Officers
President: Orlan Sawey, Texas A&I University in Kingsville
Vice-President: Ernest B. Speck, Sul Ross State University
Treasurer: Edwin W. Gaston, Jr., Stephen F. Austin State University
Secretary-Editor: Francis E. Abernethy, Stephen F. Austin State University
Councilors: Zula Vizard, Ernestine Sewell, Ralph Houston, Anne Phillips, Mary Elizabeth Nye, Bessie Pearce
Directors: James W. Lee, Wilson M. Hudson, John O. West, Francis E. Abernethy, Sidney Cox.
Paisano Advisory Board: John Q. Anderson, University of Houston; Edwin W. Gaston, Jr., Stephen F. Austin State; Norman L. McNeil, Sul Ross University
Program Chairman: Ernest B. Speck, Sul Ross State University
Local Arrangements: Mrs. L.E. Dudley, Miss McLaurin Dudley, The Abilene Study Club
Program
Friday morning session:
Chairman: James T. Bratcher, UTEP
Welcome: J.C. Hunter, Jr., Mayor of Abilene
"Way Back Home," Martha Emmons, Baylor University
"The Freep, The Barb, and the UPS: the Folklife of the Underground Newspaper," Hermes Nye, Dallas

"The Capricious Angora," Peggy Skaggs, Angelo State University
"Signature and Self-Image: a Guard against Anonymity," Robert J. Duncan, Mesquite
"Baptized on Credit: the Humor of Woody Guthrie," Terrell F. Dixon, University of Houston
"Graham (Grim) Barnett, Gunman of the Big Bend," Joe S. Graham, Sul Ross State
Friday afternoon session:
Chairman: James W. Lee, North Texas State
"O Ty Polshi: Tales of Early Polish Settlers in Texas," Ann Carpenter, Angelo State University
"From the Halls of Justice: or, the Well Watered Gate," J.T. McCullen, Texas Tech
"A Bumper Crop of Contemporary Epigrams and Proverbs," James W. Byrd, East Texas State University
"Sons and Daughters of Cheapjohn: Continuing Traditions of the Archetypal Trader," Ernestine Sewell, University of Texas at Arlington, and Charles M. Linck, East Texas State University
"Tales from Canton's First Monday," Jim R. Harris, East Texas State University
"Editorial Reaction to Blackface Minstrelsy in the Pre-Civil War South," Peter M. Stephan, Texas Tech
Dinner Toastmaster: Orlan Sawey, President
Speaker: Robert Flynn, Novelist and Playwright, "Growing up in Chillicothe, Midway, and Jackson Springs"
Saturday session:
Chairman: Conrad Dunagan, Monahans
"Wild, Wild Women: or, the Western Heroine in Dime Novels," Joyce Roach, Keller
"Jefferson Davis Tant, a Legend in His Own Time," Orlan Sawey, Texas A&I, Kingsville
"Following the Forked Stick," Archie P. McDonald, Stephen F. Austin State
"Los Pastores," Charles B. Martin, North Texas State University
"The World is Going to Pot: The Folklore of Marijuana," Robert L. Russell, The University of Texas at Austin

The Folklore of Texan Cultures. PTFS XXXVIII. Francis Edward Abernethy, ed. Austin: The Encino Press, 1974.

CONTENTS

Fifty-ninth annual meeting, Houston, March 27–29, 1975, held at the Marriott Motor Hotel, hosted by the University of Houston.

Officers

President: Ernest B. Speck, Sul Ross University

Vice President: Joyce Roach, Keller

Treasurer: Edwin W. Gaston, Jr., Stephen F. Austin University

Secretary-Editor: Francis E. Abernethy, Stephen F. Austin University

Councilors: Zula Vizard, Ernestine Sewell, Anne Phillips, Leroy Brown, Hudson Long, Robert Duncan, James Bratcher

Directors: John O. West, UTEP; Francis E. Abernethy, Stephen F. Austin University; Sid Cox, Texas A&M; Paul Patterson, Sierra Blanca; James W. Byrd, East Texas State University

Paisano Advisory Board: John Q. Anderson, University of Houston, Edwin W. Gaston, Jr., Stephen F. Austin University; Norman L. McNeil, Sul Ross University

Program Chairman: Joyce Roach, Keller

Local Arrangements: Anne R. Phillips, Chairman; Terrell F. Dixon, William Wright, Ann Lilliedahl, Helen Viereck, Mary Connelly, and Jo Lyday

Program

Thursday-Hootenanny

Friday morning session:

Chairman: Paul Patterson, Sierra Blanca

"Art Folklorica: The Designs of Guatemala," A National Bicentennial Project sponsored by the Bicentennial Association of Texas. Geoffrey Grimes, Mountain View College

"Big Thicket Legendary," Lois Williams Parker, Beaumont
"Goin' Home with the Dasypus Novemcinctus: The Mystique of the Armadillo," Hermes Nye, Dallas
"Mommanem: Some Notes on Mothers and Others," James Ward Lee, North Texas State
"Backfires and Blowouts; or, Spice in the Life of a Shade-Tree Mechanic," Palmer H. Olsen, Clifton
Friday afternoon session:
Chairman: Mary Nye, Dallas
"The Didactic Nature of Some Mexican-American Folk Tales," Joe Graham, Sul Ross State University
"Folklore and Folklife of the Mexican Cowboy at Work and Play," Nora Ramirez, San Antonio College
"Ethnic Jamboree: The Texas Folklife Festival," Charles B. Martin, North Texas State University
"The Development of Western Swing Music," Guy Logsdon, University of Tulsa
"From Billings to Baxter: The Evolution of Gospel Style," Francis E. Abernethy, Stephen F. Austin State University
"Artistic Techniques with Fiction and Fact in Three Lomax Outlaw Songs," Lawrence Clayton, Hardin-Simmons University
Dinner Toastmaster: Ernest B. Speck, President
Speaker: C.L. (Leland) Sonnichsen, the University of Arizona, "The Poor Wayfaring Scholar or Jest Lookin' fer a Home"
Saturday session:
Chairman: James M. Day, The University of Texas at El Paso
"Cobras at K-Mart, Rats at Colonel Sanders: The Nature of Today's Local Legends," Anne Carpenter, Angelo State University
"Ubiquitous Ambiguities," J.T. McCullen, Jr., Texas Tech
"Something to Crow About," Ernest Speck, Sul Ross State University
"The Folklore of Neiman-Marcus," Stanley Marcus, Dallas
Business Meeting

Some Still Do: Essays on Texas Customs. PTFS XXXIX. Francis Edward Abernethy, ed. Austin: The Encino Press, 1975.

CONTENTS

Sixtieth annual meeting, held at Arlington, April 15–17, 1976, at the Ramada Inn, hosted by the University of Texas at Arlington.
Officers
President: Joyce Roach, Keller
Vice President: Col. William H. Hardin, Houston
Treasurer: Edwin W. Gaston, Jr., Stephen F. Austin State University
Secretary-Editor: Francis E. Abernethy, Stephen F. Austin State University
Councilors: Anne Carpenter, Peter Stephen, Palmer H. Olsen, Joe Graham, Charles B. Martin, Zula Vizard, Leroy Brown, Ernestine Sewell
Directors: John O. West, UTEP; Francis Abernethy, Stephen F. Austin State University; Sid Cox, Texas A&M; Paul Patterson, Sierra Blanca; James W. Byrd, East Texas State University
Paisano Advisory Board: Edwin W. Gaston, Jr., Stephen F. Austin State University; Norman L. McNeil, Southwest Texas State University
Program Chairman: Col. William H. Hardin
Local Arrangements: Ernestine Sewell, J.C. Martin, Don Swadley, Joyce McGowan, Nancy Reid, Joyce Beck
Program
Thursday: Howdy Party, Hootenanny
Friday morning session, Chairman: Charles B. Martin, North Texas State University
Welcome: Dr. Wendell Nedderman, president, the University of Texas at Arlington
Bicentennial Greetings: Gene Brownrigg, State Chairman of the Bicentennial Commission of Texas, Arlington
"Mystery Rites of Coban Indians," Zoel Valdez Molina, Director of Folklore Studies, Guatemalan Ministry of Education
"Bilingual Folklore," John Sauvageau, Texas A&I University
"The Primary Function of Storytelling," Faye Leeper, Midland
"The Sound of Texas," Tumbleweed Smith
"Columbus Discouraged America," Archie B. McDonald, Stephen F. Austin State University
"Side Meat and Cracklin's," Ernest B. Speck, Sul Ross State University
Friday afternoon session:
Chairman: Edwin Gaston, Stephen F. Austin State University
"Curandero: An Ecological Perspective," Joe Graham, Sul Ross State University

"A Nineteenth Century UFO," Robert J. Duncan, Mesquite
"Texas Camel Folklore," James M. Day, UTEP
"Telling 'em What I'm Telling 'em," Martha Emmons, Baylor
"No Laughing Matter: Ranch Women in the Humor of the West," Joyce Roach, Keller
"From Loathly Ladies to Victimized Females," Ann Carpenter, Angelo State University
"Harlots and Hymnals: An Historic Confrontation of Vice and Virtue in Waco, Texas," Margaret Davis, Baylor University
Dinner Toastmaster: Joyce Roach, President
Speaker: Elmer Kelton, San Angelo, "Three Kinds of Truth: Fact, Folklore and Fiction"
Saturday session:
Chairman: James Ward Lee, North Texas State University
Hosted by the Library of the University of Texas at Arlington, Special Collections Department
Greetings: J.C. Martin, Director, the Jenkins Garrett Library
"Pearling and Pier Breaks: The Folksay of the Surf Rider," Hermes Nye, Dallas
"From Buffalo Hide to Acrylics: Indian Art," Ernestine P. Sewell, U.T. at Arlington, and Charles E. Linck, East Texas State University
"Ben K. Green: A Panel"
Moderator: James Byrd, East Texas State University
Panelists: A.C. Greene, Dallas; Margaret Hartley, S.M.U. Press; Art Hendrix, East Texas State University; Frank X. Tolbert, Dallas; Robert A. Wilson, Dallas
Some Final Remarks: Jenkins Garrett, Fort Worth
Business Meeting

What's Going On? (In Modern Texas Folklore). PTFS XL. Francis Edward Abernethy, ed. Austin: The Encino Press, 1976.

CONTENTS

Sixty-first annual meeting, held at El Paso, April 7–9, 1977, jointly with the New Mexico Folklore Society.

Officers

President: William H. Hardin, Houston

Vice-President: Ernestine Sewell, Arlington

Secretary-Editor: Francis E. Abernethy, Nacogdoches

Treasurer: Edwin W. Gaston, Jr., Nacogdoches

Directors: Sid Cox, College Station; Paul Patterson, Sierra Blanca; James W. Byrd, Commerce; Martha Emmons, Waco; Ernest Speck, Alpine

Councilors: Anne Carpenter, San Angelo; Palmer H. Olsen, Clifton; Joe Graham, Alpine; Charles B. Martin, Denton; Zula Vizard, San Antonio; Peter Stephan, Lubbock; Leroy Brown, Galveston

Program Coordinators: Ernestine Sewell, Rosa Fernandez

Local Arrangements: James M. Day, John O. West, D. J. Day, Jean Eberle, Don Eberle, Joey Day, David Tuck, Deane Mansfield-Kelley

Program

Thursday: Registration, Hootenanny

Friday morning first session:

Welcome: James K.P. Mortensen, University of Texas El Paso

Presiding: Joseph Leach, University of Texas El Paso

"The Folklore of Hand Signs," T.M. Pearce, University of New Mexico

"Clanging Church Chime Cuentos," Benito Cordova, Pan American University

"Religious Folklore in Hispanic New Mexico," Carmen Gertrudis Espinoza, Albuquerque

"Endless Search for Sources of a WPA Song," Jenny Wells Vincent, San Cristobal, New Mexico

Second session (Friday morning):

Presiding: Charles Linck, East Texas State University

"Compadrazgo: A Tradition Changes But Survives," Joe Graham, Sul Ross State University

"'Gabby, Round Up Some of the Boys': The Sidekick in the Western Movie," James Ward Lee, North Texas State University

"New Day at Noonday: Continuing Studies of Campmeetings," Melvin R. Mason, Sam Houston State University

"'In a Narrow Grave . . . ' Lomax's Dying Cowboys, Rangers, and Soldiers," Lawrence Clayton, Hardin-Simmons University
"Oh Bury Me Not Piece by Piece," Ernest B. Speck, Sul Ross State University
Business Meeting, New Mexico Folklore Society: Muriel Latham-Pfeiffer, President, presiding
Third Session:
Presiding: Ray Past, University of Texas, El Paso
"Growing Up in a Folklore-Deprived Community," Ernest W. Baughman, University of New Mexico
"Meaningless Refrains in Folk Songs," John Donald Robb, University of New Mexico
"Indian Slavery and Peonage in New Mexico," Robert Torres, Los Ojos, New Mexico
"The Changing Compadrazgo in Mexican Immigrants in the United States," Silvester John Brito, University of Wisconsin
Fourth session:
Presiding: Martha Emmons, Waco
"Folklore in the Age of the Ford," James W. Byrd, East Texas State University
"Highland Games at Grandfather Mountain," Charles Martin, North Texas State University
"The Captain of Castroville: A Graveyard Legend," Terri Ross, Abilene
"Tall Dark Strangers and Mysterious Journeys: The Folklore of the Tarot Cards," Hermes Nye, Dallas
"Meanwhile, Back in Transylvania, or Dracula and the Texan," Sylvia Grider, Texas A&M
Banquet Welcome: William H. Hardin, President, Texas Folklore Society
Response: Muriel Latham-Pfeifer, President, New Mexico Folklore Society
Address: T.M. Pearce, "Reminiscences of the 1938 Joint Meeting of the New Mexico and Texas Folklore Societies,"
Program: Rosa Guerrero, El Paso, "Cultural Confluence Through Dance"
Fifth session, Saturday:
Presiding: Haldeen Braddy, UTEP
"Oil Field Anecdotes from Llano Estacado," Jim Harris, New Mexico Junior College
"Lorenzo Delgado: A Case Study of a New Mexico Hispanic Patron Politico," Paul Roybal, Las Vegas, New Mexico
"History and Folklore in Analog: Smoking the Comanches Out of Truchas," William de Buys, Chamiza, New Mexico
"New Mexico Health Practices: Home Remedies, Beliefs and Superstitions," Elvira G. Cobos, Albuquerque
Sixth session, Saturday:
Presiding: Don Swadley, U.T. at Arlington
"Sex and the Old Time Cowboy," Paul Patterson, Crane, Texas
"Folk Motifs in Hands Around the World: The Republic of South Korea," Geoffrey A. Grimes, Mountain View Community College
"The Captive Narrative," Glen E. Lich, Southwest Texas State University
"Illustrating the Dobie Books and Stories: The Artist's Recollections," Ben Carlton Mead, Dallas

Business meeting, Texas Folklore Society, William H. Hardin, President, presiding.
Seventh session 7:15 p.m. Saturday:
Informal eating and shopping tour in Ciudad Juarez, Chihuahua

Sixty-second annual meeting, held at Nacogdoches, March 23–25, 1978, at the Fredonia Inn. Hosted by Stephen F. Austin State University.
Officers
President: Ernestine Sewell, Arlington
Vice-President: James M. Day, El Paso
Secretary-Editor: Francis E. Abernethy, Nacogdoches
Treasurer: Edwin W. Gaston, Jr., Nacogdoches
Directors: Paul Patterson, Sierra Blanca; James W. Byrd, Commerce; Martha Emmons, Waco; Ernest Speck, Alpine; Geoffrey Grimes, Dallas
Councilors: Jack Duncan, Mesquite; Lawrence Clayton, Abilene; Sylvia Grider, College Station; Ann Carpenter, San Angelo; Palmer H. Olsen, Clifton; Joe Graham, Alpine; Charles B. Martin, Denton; Peter Stephan, Lubbock
Program Chairman: James M. Day, U.T. El Paso
Local Arrangements: Edwin Gaston, Archie McDonald, Pat Barton, R.G. Dean, Willie Earl Tindall, Hazel Abernethy, Martha Dickson
Program
Thursday: Registration, Autograph party, Barbeque and Hootenanny at Fern Lake
Friday, first session:
Presiding: Peter Stephan, Lubbock
"Verbal Folk Humor as a Structural Device in Brando's One-Eyed Jacks," Jim Harris, Hobbs, New Mexico
"A Key of Golden—Some Teaching Experiences," Mrs. John Q. Anderson, Ruston, Louisiana
"Pull Rings, Kidney Machines and the Oral Tradition," Lawrence Clayton, Abilene
Second session:
Presiding: Charles Linck, Commerce
"Bull Adams, The Paluxy Eccentric," Robert J. Duncan, Mesquite
"Modern Nomads," Archie P. McDonald, Nacogdoches
"Folk Motifs in Hands Around the World: Ireland," Geoffrey A. Grimes, DeSoto
Third session:
Presiding: Bill Hardin, Austin
"The Boarding House, or Secession in the Piney Woods," Martha Emmons, Waco
"Notes for a Final Section of Mody Boatright's Cowboy as Hero," Ernest Speck, Alpine
"I Never Knew a Texan until . . . " Emory C. Whipple, Fort Wayne, Indiana
Fourth session:
Presiding: Claudia Ball, San Antonio

"The Newton Boys: Portrait of an Outlaw Gang," David L. Middleton, San Antonio (film)
Banquet speaker: Julya Kirkpatrick, "Old Houses in Texas"
Hoot: After banquet
Fifth session:
Presiding: Lou Rodenberger, Bryan
"Folkloring in the San Antonio Produce Market," Alice Sessions, El Paso
"Mules in Texas," Suzy Schoener-Lozoya, Bryan
"Joshua Beene and Jewel Gibson," Martha Anne Turner, Huntsville
Business meeting
Sixth session:
Presiding: Glen Lich, San Marcos
"Bob Wills and Folk Music," Rex Wilson, Alpine
"The Tenacious Texas Tick," R.L. Cowser, Jr., Wharton
"The Glamour of the Gay Night Life: The Typical Texas Honky Tonk," James W. Lee, Denton

Paisanos: A Folklore Miscellany. PTFS XLI. Francis Edward Abernethy, editor. Austin, The Encino Press, 1978.

CONTENTS

James Snyder, illustrator for *Observations and Reflections*

Linda Roach, illustrator for *Paisanos*

Joseph and Johanna Jones. In 1979 Joe made Boatright's Bodark, the Society's official gavel and knocker block, from bois d'arc that he retrieved from Mody Boatright's workshop.

Pehl's Old Time Band playing for the banquet dance in Fredericksburg, 1982

Bill Brett, hog hunter and story teller from the Big Thicket

Hootenanny in full cry, Arlington, 1976

Joe Lomax and Hallie Wood

John O. West, Jo Lyday, Joyce Roach Jim McNutt, and Jim Harris —a panel on urban folklore

Rhett, Marlene, and Paul Rushing

David LaRo

John O. West and Brenda Black White with a Boatright paisano

Bruce Ayars

Rosemary and Walter Killam

Kent Biffle of the *Dallas Morning News*, Sarah Greene of the *Gilmer Mirror*, and Dick Potter, Professor of Pos-sumology

Martha Mitchell, Texas quiltmaker

Kenneth Munson, "dancin' Josie!"

Mary Elizabeth Nye, hostess at Fredericksburg

Lucille Enix

Lora B. Garrison

Art Hendrix

Karen Haile & Dawn Cox

Mike Cox

Al Lowman

George and Zula Vizard, Milton McAfee, Dawn Cox, Deurelle McAfee, and Bill Stokes

Kenneth Munson leads a Josie party dance

Lee and Karen Haile with daughters Acayla and Sierra

Old John's girls, Bess Lomax Hawes and Shirley Lomax Duggen, harmonizing in Huntsville, 1984

Martha Anne Turner and Melvin Mason

Ernest Speck, Bill Cox, Paul Patterson, and David LaRo

Glen Lich

In October 1997 a Mexican working on Glen Lich's ranch near Kerrville, lured Glen away from the house claiming that there was an emergency of some sort. The Mexican later returned to the house, overcame Glen's wife Lera, and tied her up. He demanded ten thousand dollars ransom. Getting no money, he left, and Lera was able to escape and call the police. Glen was found that same morning, bludgeoned to death. The Mexican illegal, Ramiro Hernandez, a murderer who had escaped from the Matamoros jail, was later caught and jailed.

Glen Lich was a kind and gentle man and a scholar. His smile brought warmth to all around him. Glen was a historian and an author. He founded the Hill Country Institute and taught at Baylor, where he was the Director of Regional Studies. Among many other publications, Glen wrote *The German Texans*, much of which was about his own German ancestry, and he edited *German Culture in Texas* for the Twayne Series.

Glen was a richness and a treasure in the Society.

II
E-Heart and SMU Press: 1979 to 1989

"Looking for love in all the wrong places"...
URBAN COWBOY
ARE YOU BETTER OFF TODAY THAN YOU WERE 4 YEARS AGO?

1979

James M. Day
President 1978–79 at Waco
Professor Emeritus of English at University of Texas at El Paso, former Director of El Paso Centennial Museum, former Director of State Archives, Texas historian and author of *Captain Clint Peoples, Texas Ranger*

Even though *Built in Texas* was the publication of the Texas Folklore Society for 1979, it was built—written and illustrated—in Texas in 1978. No book is closer to this editor-photographer-writer's heart than *Built in Texas*, and mainly that is because I learned so much while I was building it. I traveled all over this state. The Ford pickup—which I swapped this year for a 2000 model—was eight years old then and just broken in. I made several big trips during the summer of 1978 studying barns and houses, fences, windmills, and stock ponds. My first trip was up through the blacklands, over the Cross Timbers, and then through the Panhandle. My second trip was out to Fort Stockton, Alpine, and Presidio to study adobe buildings. I remember calling Hazel on that trip and telling her that I had paid fifty-four cents a gallon for gasoline! On a third trip I nearly wore out my camera shooting those great German rock houses in the Hill Country. I took another swing down through Corpus, the Valley, and Laredo.

I camped out most of the time. The weather was Texas summer hot, so I usually sacked out in the pickup bed under the starry skies. I got caught in the rain a couple of times. On such occasions I would back up to a tree, tie a lariat from the tree across the top of the cab to the front bumper and throw a tarpaulin over it. That made a good tent.

I enjoyed the photography. I am convinced that looking through a view finder focuses both mind and intellect on the object more than just looking will. I know that these and other shorter trips taught me more about Texas and buildings and human beings as builders than I can ever realize. My interest in photography prompted me to send out a call to all TFS photographers for illustrations for *Legendary Ladies of Texas* and other upcoming publications.

Built in Texas was an education in more ways than one. This was the first outsize book that the Society had ever published since Bill Owens' *Texas Folk Songs* (PTFS 23–1950). Forty publications had been bound in the standard six-by-nine-inch size. Now we came along with an oversize longways book that would not fit into the standard book rack. Some members protested.

Also, *Built in Texas* cost a bundle. The total cost of three thousand volumes was $27,673.81. The Society began 1979 with $21,007.19, before bills were paid. We received $8850 in grants, but the records show that we paid E-Heart only $8000. Fran sold some more cows and carried the rest of the cost of the book, finally clearing costs and making $2,469.20 by April 1980. If the Vick family had relied on E-Heart Press for groceries that year, they would have eaten light.

But we did other things than get a book out that year of 1979.

We met with the Baylor Baptists at Waco at the Sheraton Inn, April 12–14, 1979, with James M. Day, Professor of English at the University of Texas at El Paso, presiding. That year marked the Society's seventieth anniversary, and President Day made the Waco meeting "an Event." For Thursday night, the members took an evening riverboat cruise on the Brazos. For the Friday night banquet, James Day presented scrolls to all the living past presidents of the Society. The main award that night was the Grasshopper Library Award, which he presented to Martha Emmons, the Society's grande dame, whose membership went back to 1924. The award scroll was an original by José Cisneros of El Paso. The Grasshopper Library Award title was taken from a hymn to universal wisdom that Frank Dobie included in *Coronado's Children*: ". . . in the wide-spreading Grasshopper's Library I have learned the most valuable things I know" (Preface, xi).

Bob Collmer, that year's local arranger and Baylor's English department head, announced that evening the publication of a festschrift honoring E. Hudson Long, another longtime TFS member.

On the nomination of President James M. Day, John Q. Anderson (1916–1975) was accepted by the Board of Directors and voted by the membership as a Fellow of the Texas Folklore Society, the award to be posthumously presented at the 1980 meeting in San Antonio.

Also at the banquet, Joseph Jones presented President Day the official gavel and knocker block which Jones had made out of some bois d'arc that Mody Boatright had left him. The gavel was appropriately called Boatright's Bodark, and we are still using it. Joe, a professor of English at UT, wrote on January 12, 1979: "I have in my shop a piece of bodark, as we would say, that came out of Mody Boatright's shop; Art Cory [one-time TFS Treasurer], in fact, was the man who got it and passed it along to me, sort of on shares. It's well-seasoned heartwood, plenty big enough to make a head and handle for just about any gavel we might require, I'd say. Any artifact made of this particular piece of bodark could be called, in full apostolic legitimacy, 'Boatright's Bodark,' which I would think might be a pretty good name for what we contemplate." A month later (letter to editor February 24, 1979) the gavel was finished, and Joe wrote: "'Boatright's Bodark' complete with knock-block as holder now hangs on my study wall and is ready for instant service. . . . [I]t makes an imperative noise, which I suppose is its chief function, as seems to be true of lots of other things, and people."

Two other distinct memories of the Waco meeting stay with me. We went to the Armstrong Browning Library and stood reverently before the bronze hands of Elizabeth and Robert as if this icon were the true cross itself. And I am still in shock from a session chairman's calling time on a program reader and then talking himself for fifteen minutes or more. That incident caused the Society to institute a ruling that the chairman's remarks could not be longer than the paper he was introducing.

For the first time, in 1979 the Texas Folklore Society provided a folklore session for the annual meeting of the Texas State Historical Association. Jim Lee, Sylvia Grider, and I were the presenters, and because so many folklorists are also historians we had a full house. And since then, I am proud to say, the TFS session at TSHA has regularly filled the house and provided Texas historians with some of their most interesting and exciting sessions.

Ayatollah Ruhollah Khomeini, the Imam of the Islamic Republic of Iran, is the marker for the year of 1979. Khomeni came to power with the deposition of Shah Mohammed Reza Pahlavi and began a hate campaign against the United States that has not yet subsided. One result was that on November 4, 1979, Iranian militants stormed and captured the U. S. Embassy in Tehran and imprisoned fifty-two U. S. citizens. The Iranians demanded that we return the Shah, who was then in the States for medical treatment. The hostages were held through 1979 and 1980. They were freed minutes after Ronald Reagan was sworn in as president of the United States. The episode was an ultimate embarrassment—similar to the 1968 Pueblo incident in North Korea—the world's superpower being held at the mercy of a small third-world country.

Fran Vick, publisher and director of E-Heart Press

1980

Robert J. (Jack) Duncan
President 1979–80 at San Antonio
Editorial Manager for Retractable Technologies, Inc., Adjunct English professor at Grayson County College, and professional free-lance writer published in *Reader's Digest, True West* and *Chicken Soup for the Country Soul*

The Iranians still had the United States by the short hairs in 1980, and we compounded our international embarrassment with a botched commando rescue raid. Mount St. Helens erupted and killed everything within a 155 square-mile area. And folklorically—pop-culturally—John Travolta in *Urban Cowboy* began a Texas-style dressing trend that lasted long enough for boot, belt, and cowboy hat makers to prosper for a decade. Windows draped with western paraphernalia in posh New York and London stores was a sight to behold.

The Society, with Jack Duncan of McKinney as president, met that spring with Claudia Ball and the Institute of Texan Cultures in San Antonio. Claudia was the director of the Texas Folklife Festival at the time and had the run of the Institute. Jack was then laboratory manager for St. Regis Paper Company and is now a professional free-lance writer with an enviable record of national publications.

Claudia's initiative and expertise, in fact, saved us from a very embarrassing situation. Both President Duncan and Secretary Abernethy showed up at the banquet without a scroll to present for John Q. Anderson's investment as a Fellow of the Society.

Claudia descended into the bowels of the ITC building and emerged soon after with a frameable scroll that would have done justice to the Printer himself. John Q. was formally and posthumously inducted: "In recognition of his many years of distinguished service as member, officer and contributor to the Texas Folklore Society and particularly as a renowned national scholar and author in the field of folklore and in the Society's sincere appreciation of his leadership, scholarship, and friendship, John Q. Anderson (1916–1975) is hereby designated Fellow of the Texas Folklore Society. Awarded at Waco, Texas, April 14, 1979, Presented at San Antonio, Texas, April 4, 1980." Above and beyond the formal phrases, John Q. was the leader in the revitalization of the Society during the slow time of the 1950s. He deserved the Fellowship.

We had some seminal papers at that year's meeting. Al Lowman gave his "Pissing on Elephant Ears" paper, which was the beginning of his saga of the Lowman family in Staples, Texas. Robert Flynn gave the banquet address, "Growing Up a Sullen Baptist," which has been on the boards in one form or another ever since and is still a hilarious twenty minutes from the speaker's stand.

The Guatemala American Studies Conference for 1980 featured the Texas Folklore Society and speakers therefrom. The Conference met in Guatemala City from June 27 to July 6, 1980, and the Texas part was under the guidance of Geoffrey Grimes of DeSoto, director of the Texas Cultural Alliance. We presented our papers in Spanish. The East Texas String Ensemble went along and provided the musical background.

Legendary Ladies of Texas, the book scheduled for 1980, hit various sorts of snags and did not make press in time for 1980 publication. The Society, therefore, went with Riley Aiken's *Mexican Folktales from the Borderland* (ExB 17–1980), an SMU Press book. Riley was an old-time Paisano in the Society, and the stories from Mexican Folktales came from his contributions to the Society's publications from *Puro Mexicano* (PTFS 12) in 1935 to *A Good Tale and a Bonnie Tune* (PTFS 32) in 1964. Riley, who was raised among border Mexicans, had known the stories from his youth, and during his studentship at The University he took them to J. Frank Dobie, who promptly included them in the Society's publication.

Fran Vick moved the headquarters of E-Heart Press to 3700 Mockingbird Lane in Dallas in 1980. Our correspondence reflected that the publisher spent most of the year working on *Legendary Ladies* and redoing the kitchen in her new Dallas house.

That was the year, 1980, that William N. Stokes, a noted lawyer from Dallas and the Society's Counselor and legal advisor, suggested that we start binding copies of the papers presented at the spring meetings. And most importantly, Bill offered to pay for the binding. The board quickly accepted the offer, and for some reason, that year the papers were sent to President Lawrence Clayton to collect, organize, and send to the binder. Lawrence had just been installed as the first Dean of the College of Arts and Sciences at Hardin-Simmons. He sent the papers to Library Binders in Waco, and the first set of papers was bound. The binding was red, and we have since followed a pattern of red, blue, green. Bill Stokes' idea has been a help to the TFS editor, since he has all of the papers in hand from which to prepare the miscellanies. Bill has continued to pay for each binding and has since established an endowment that will pay for future bindings. The Society is truly thankful for such members.

John Q. Anderson (1916–1975), Fellow of the Texas Folklore Society, 1980

1981

Lawrence R. Clayton
President 1980–81 at Denton
Dean of the College of Arts & Sciences at Hardin-Simmons University, rancher, west Texas writing includes books on Elmer Kelton and Ben Capps and *Historic Ranches of Texas* and *Longhorn Legacy*

This year should not be very hard to remember. Ronald Reagan was sworn in as president; and on the same day, as the ultimate insult to Jimmy Carter, Iran freed the fifty-two American hostages. That was the year that Egypt's Anwar Sadat was assassinated, and Ronald Reagan and Pope John Paul II were both severely wounded by would-be assassains. On a more ephemeral note, Prince Charles and Lady Diana married and *Raiders of the Lost Ark* hit the screen.

We met at the Holiday Inn in Denton on April 16–18, 1981, with Lawrence Clayton of Hardin-Simmons, Abilene, presiding. In addition to being a dean, Lawrence is a rancher who writes about west Texas ranch life.

I am sure that we had a fine set of papers at Denton, but my main memory is of Jerry Duke clog dancing on a table as he delivered his. His dancing was amazing, but even more so was the fact that the table did not collapse. We also had home movies of the TFS-Guatemala program of the year before, and the East Texas String Ensemble played at the hootenanny.

Charles Martin's main memory, and Charles was the program chairman that year, was that he had scheduled the Voices of Praise, a black choir from Denton, to sing after the banquet. On Friday morning of the banquet he was informed that most of the singers had gone home for the Easter holiday weekend and the choir would be unable to perform. Charles miraculously found a jazz guitarist and a bass player, who put Voices of Praise in the shade. Charles' next surprise came when he walked into the meeting room on Saturday morning to check on the p. a. system. The room had been arranged as a night club and was completely trashed out with the detritus of a previous night's party. He and the girl at the front desk put it in TFS meeting order in twenty minutes. Charles survived.

Two changes occurred in the machinery of the TFS in 1981. Hermes Nye, hootenanny leader and legal advisor, died that year, and William N. Stokes was appointed by the board as Society Counselor. And Martha Dickson, the Society's secretary resigned her position. Martha had been secretary ever since the TFS moved from Austin to Nacogdoches, and she knew more about the business than I did. She kept books, wrote letters, edited, and did a lot of everything to keep the Society running smoothly. Martha was irreplaceable.

To compound the chaos following Martha's resignation, we had four books under way in the office during 1981. I was still working on *Legendary Ladies* that spring. Additionally, I was putting together a traditional miscellany for the upcoming year, 1982, and I was frantically calling for papers and pictures for the folk art book that was scheduled for 1983. In my spare time I was working on *Singin' Texas*.

The book that Society members got in 1981 was *Legendary Ladies of Texas* (PTFS 43). The Society produced that book in conjunction with the Texas Foundation for Women's Resources. Mary Beth Rogers was Project Director of the Texas Foundation, and my original intent was to make *Legendary Ladies* a joint project of our two groups, with the Foundation paying $5000 of production costs, about one-third of the total cost. As it worked out, the Society did get some help from the Foundation with articles for the book, but no money was forthcoming.

Legendary Ladies was a long time in the making. Ege Wray of Austin did the layout, and Fran Vick and I were both very pleased with the results of her artistic eye, but not with her speed. Ege was not to be hurried. So the books finally got to members in August of 1981.

Legendary Ladies made a big splash. The book had good reviews in the state's major newspapers, Fran and I did radio talk-show interviews, and on November 8, 1981, we had a big book signing party at the Hall of State in Dallas with most of the contributors present.

One problem, however, arose. Martha Anne Turner's essay on Emily Morgan was supposed to be a summary article from her previously published *The Yellow Rose of Texas: Her Saga and Her Song*. She had signed a release to that effect. It was not far enough from the original text, however, to satisfy her publsher, W. L. Thompson of Shoal Creek Publishers in Austin. In a letter to Fran dated September 14, 1981, Mr. Thompson said, "We feel that the use of our literary property in 'Legendary Ladies of Texas' is a positive infringement, and that all copies of 'Legendary Ladies of Texas' should be recalled and promptly destroyed." Needless to say, that started the phones to ringing. We spent a month with our Counselor Bill Stokes, other lawyers, and many letters and phone calls, and finally reached an agreement. On the advice of Counselor Stokes I sent a notarized statement disclaiming any use of the article beyond its present use and guaranteeing Shoal Creek's publication and film rights. Fran printed a statement identifying the Shoal Creek source for insertion in all future *Legendary Ladies* publications. We smoked the peace pipe with Mr. Thompson on October 6, 1981. That had been a long and harried month!

We ended 1981 with a balance of $28,837.85, down by $3,219.95 from 1980, but still doing better than we ever had in the sixty-five years of TFS existence.

1982

Charles B. Martin
President 1981–1982 at Fredericksburg
Professor of English at University of North Texas (retired), world traveler, photographer, linguist

The Society met in Fredericksburg in 1982. That was the first time in recent decades that the TFS had met without university sponsorship and financing. Local arrangers were usually college folk who were able to get five hundred dollars, more or less, from their institutions in return for the honor of sponsorship. In the early years of the Society, the meetings were held on campuses. By the 1950s the Society had adopted the practice of meeting in a hotel where they could do everything in one place and not spend time wandering about campuses. And here we were wandering about in Fredericksburg, a town that did not even have a college.

Hermes and Mary Elizabeth Nye had decided that they wanted to have a meeting in Fredericksburg before Hermes died. Mary Elizabeth saw to it that it happened. With the help of the Fredericksburg Chamber of Commerce and the J. B. Hutchinsons, Elizabeth made the local arrangements. Because we had no institutional money, we charged a two-dollar registration fee, the first time that we had ever done that. The financial arrangements worked out all right, however, and after paying all the bills, the Society was twenty dollars in the black.

Arranging the meeting place was a trying experience. The Best Western Sunday House Motel was the only place large enough to handle our size convention. I wrote them for rates and received a sheet with a $29 and $33 base rate listed. On our first exchange of letters, the manager raised the price to $31 and $33, saying that I was looking at the previous year's rates. And before we had finished arrangements, he had gone up again to $33 and $37, saying that he thought we were booking as a group when he gave us the other prices. By this time I was apoplectic, but had already announced the place of meeting. We met at the Sunday House in Fredericksburg, had an as-usual good meeting, and I never did see the manager, which was just as well.

Charles Martin, world traveler and Professor of English at North Texas State University, presided at this sixty-sixth annual meeting. We had the Friday session in the Fredericksburg Library and met Saturday at the Sunday House. Lee Haile, a student of Sylvia Grider's at Texas A&M, completely charmed the members with his paper on and demonstration of Texas folk toys. Lee's paper was the inspiration for *Texas Toys and Games* (PTFS 48–1989), and Lee's picture was on the cover. And after the Friday night banquet Pehl's Old Time Band played Fredericksburg-German music for a dance.

The book for 1982 was a miscellany entitled *T for Texas: A State Full of Folklore* (PTFS 44). I celebrated my tenth anniversary as Secretary-Editor that year, and I got together the very best papers over the past four years for this book. I also put in the preface a brief history of the Society and my philosophy of folklore. I began: "I've had this job ten years now and I'm still impressed with it. I've hunted some big bucks, caught some fine fish, and played some great gigs, but nothing in my professional life has been as important to me as the Texas Folklore Society and the welfare of its members." In the year 2000 I still feel that way.

Farther on in the preface I summarize my philosophy of folklore:

"The major work of preserving and presenting folklore in Texas has from its beginning centered in the Texas Folklore Society. The development of departments, divisions, and centers in universities has not significantly changed this because the academic approach, even though it has preserved, has not been successful in its presenting. As I look back over the Society's history I find that the period of time when folklore received its greatest attention and had the greatest effect in making people conscious of the infinite variety and richness of their culture was the time when it was least associated with academicians, during the 'twenties and 'thirties of J. Frank Dobie. Academicians, of which I consider myself one, are the brightest lights which a civilization shines, but they are prone to dabble in esoterica and pedantry, and to dwell in a rarified atmosphere that relates but poorly to the general public. So, professional folklorists may cuss the Dobies and Botkins and Foxfires and picture books by *Life* and *National Geographic* for their sometimes creative approach to their subject, but these are the forces that have focused the public eye on folklore, and these are the forces that have made the public conscious through folklore of the beauty and richness of their culture.

"I conclude with an examination, or more accurately, a statement of the Texas Folklore Society's direction as I see it.

"I believe that the Society's main purpose is to search for ways to preserve folklore without embalming it and to present a fairly well-educated public with the treasures of their culture's folk life. I do not believe that our purpose is to proliferate esoterica and pedantry among a small, specially educated clique. I further believe that the Texas Folklore Society's purpose is to preserve and present the folklore of Texas. This does not mean that our purpose is to be chauvinistic or provincial, both of which are brought about by states of mind rather than geographical locations. It means, as Kittredge said so many years ago, that Texas really is the folklorist's happy hunting ground, that we have all the fields we can ever plow, and that the work and the room to work is as wide as its borders and as inexhaustible as the winds that blow across the Staked Plains. And this work should be done by those who know the land and love it and understand it. And finally, I believe that the purpose of the Texas Folklore Society is not to hide the light of the lore under a bushel of academic guidelines and definitions and scholarly verbiage but to let that light so shine among men that all the world—but, Lord, most especially Texans—may see the richness of the land and its people and its history and its continuity. In this land and its people and its history Texans must realize the place of their belonging, a mother land to moisten with their sweat, and finally to nourish with their bones."

T for Texas was as rich a collection of essays on folklore as we have ever produced. It contained papers from the major members of the Society at that time. The preface carried a fairly complete history of the TFS, and the conclusion was the "Chronological and Bibliographical Listings of the Texas Folklore Society Publications" by Herbert C. Arbuckle III, of Corpus Christi. This was a complete book which looked great on the outside. But on the inside the layout person went completely berserk, defied all artistic and editorial logic, and gave us a work that still makes me cringe when I look at it. And I was to blame. Our layout person had done such a good job on *Legendary Ladies* that I figured she would do the same with *T for Texas,* and I did not take the time to look at the blue-line copy before the book went to the printer. I was in too big a panic, trying to get the book out on time. When the finished books arrived at my office, I looked at the first copy in disbelief and disappointment and flung it across the room, where it lay for several weeks before I could bring myself to look at it again. Going through it now, I am still unable to understand how it could have been so perversely laid out, unless it was done in anger or for vengeance.

I scrambled around rather awkwardly after Martha Dickson resigned as our secretary. Then Elizabeth Young came in, took over, and handled affairs beautifully through 1982 and the spring of '83. I did not have to learn how important an experienced secretary is to the smooth running of an institution; I already knew.

Willie Earl Tindall, who gave the beer-and-barbecue at the Nacogdoches meeting

1983

Sylvia Grider
President 1982–83 at College Station
Associate Professor of Anthropology at Texas A&M University, past president of the American Folklore Society, Dorothy Scarborough scholar, co-editor of *Texas Women Writers: A Tradition of their Own.*

A big wind and dust storm hit on Saturday morning during the Easter meeting at College Station in 1983. It lifted part of the roof off of the Ramada Inn, our meeting place, and was so vicious that the management asked us not to go into the glass-covered atrium for our coffee break.

Sylvia Grider, Professor of English, folklore, and history at Texas A&M, was president for the 1983 meeting on March 31–April 2. Sylvia followed her TFS presidency with tenure in the same office for the American Folklore Society. Joe Graham of A&M gave a paper on Aggie traditions and folklore that was a memorable highlight. John Graves, of *Goodbye to a River* and *Hard Scrabble,* was the banquet speaker. He talked about his uses of folklore in his writing and delighted the membership with the warmth of his personality. John's presence also got the Society some statewide publicity. Mary Nye arranged a tour of Elizabet Ney's Liendo Plantation, near Hempstead, on Saturday afternoon.

The most dramatic event of the meeting was raising the dues to $15 single, $20 family, $30 patron, and $50 paisano grande. This was a necessary but traumatic move, considering my Depression-conditioned mentality. I hemmed and hawed about our finances, until Leroy Brown (not known for his patience) said,

"Ab, do you want to raise the dues or not? If you do, say so, and we'll do it." I said so and the members did it without half as much reluctance as I had displayed. Fifteen dollars evidently was a practical number; we continued adding to our savings and we continued profitably producing books. We have not raised dues since then, and we entered the new millennium financially stable.

The book for that year was the editor's *Singin' Texas* (ExB–18). It was an old and much changed book by the time E-Heart decided to publish it. *Singin' Texas* got started in 1967, when James Ward Lee was building his great Southwest Writers Series with Steck-Vaughn Company in Austin. I had finished the J. Frank Dobie monograph, and Lee decided to branch out from Southwest authors and do a pamphlet on Texas and Southwestern folk music. I had been working with various kinds of Texas folk music, so I started putting something together. It was not what either one of us—particularly Lee—wanted, so that manuscript was laid aside. In its dormant state that first manuscript was joined by other articles on Sacred Harp and gospel music, Josie parties, children's games, and cowboy songs, most of which were originally programs that I had given at one place or another. Thus, by the 1980s I had an accumulation of chapters on various kinds of Texas music that could be brought together in one book. After six long months in New York, it was bounced by a major publisher, so after a long evening of counseling and evaluations with Fran and her brother, Joe Pat, I revised it again. E-Heart put it together in 1983 as *Singin' Texas*. Ross Vick III, who at the time was deeply involved in the music world, cut a tape of my versions of most of the songs in the book, and we packaged tape and book and mailed them to members as the Extra Book for 1983.

Singin' Texas was another book I enjoyed building. Most of the songs were ones I had grown up listening to on my grandfather's ranch on the Washita or were a part of my East Texas raising. They were all songs that I sang and enjoyed and were my basic musical vocabulary. And they still are.

I do not know how I made it through 1983. I am very dependent on a seasoned secretary in the office to hold the Society together. In 1983 I had four secretaries! The first one was just passing through, I found. The second one came in one morning when I was frantically trying to get something together; she took a coffee break and never returned. The third was sweet and eager but absolutely unable. The fourth was Marlene Adams, who was bright and beautiful and served the Society well for the next two years.

That was the year, 1983, that the U. S. invaded Grenada, and I have forgotten why, if I ever knew.

Marlene Adams, office secretary from 1983 to 1985

1984

Charles E. Linck
President 1983–84 at Huntsville
Professor Emeritus of Literature at Texas A&M University at Commerce, Evelyn Waugh and Navaho Indian scholar, director of the Cow Hill Press, author of *Edgar Rye, North Central Texas Cartoonist and Journalist* (1972)

Melvin Mason hosted the 1984 meeting in Huntsville at the Sam Houston State University Hotel, April 19–21. Charles Linck, Professor of English at East Texas State University, Commerce—He of the coats of many colors!—presided. Charles is an Evelyn Waugh scholar who, with his Cow Hill Press, has strayed off into a folkier, Texas-cowboy world under the inspiration of Paul Patterson. The Huntsville meeting began with the President Charles and first lady Ernestine Sewell's wine-and-cheese reception and book signing for Society authors. That evening concluded with a traditional hootenanny, this one dedicated to Martha Emmons, who gave her spirited "Adulteration of Ole King David."

The editor and the Society had been working on the folk art book since 1982, so folk art was the emphasis for the program on Saturday morning, with eight papers on the subject. Pat Jasper came with several friends with papers on folk art and, as I was to find out later, a book in progress on folk art. Pat's group was the nucleus for Texas Folklife Resources, which has become a major finder, preserver, and promoter of folk artists in Texas. At this Easter meeting, the Texas Folklore Society agreed to act as the sponsor for the establishment of Texas Folklife Resources. They were applying for a grant from the National Endowment for the

Humanities and needed the Society to act as their umbrella organization.

The Huntsville meeting was highlighted by the presence of Bess Lomax Hawes, our banquet speaker, and Shirley Lomax Duggan, daughters of TFS founder John A. Lomax. Bess was the Director of the Folk Arts Program, National Endowment for the Arts.

At the business meeting Director Lawrence Clayton passed a resolution that at every annual meeting the TFS president would call a meeting of the Board of Directors and Councilors to consider nominations, meeting sites, Society finances, and other necessaries. Included in this was an institution of registration fees. This was an attempt to get members more closely involved in the running of the Society. The Board has been meeting regularly since then.

The Board also requested that TFS charter, by-laws, and significant resolutions be published in the June minutes. This was done (July 10, 1984).

The June minutes included: "John O. West and Jack Duncan suggested that the Society publish the records of the meetings held since the beginnings, with program cover art where practical." This suggestion caused the editor to begin work on this present history.

In the fall of 1983 after *Singin' Texas* came out, Fran called me one day and told me that she was going to have to abandon the publishing business in order to get her own business back in the black. This meant that I would have to find another publisher for *Folk Art in Texas*, the 1984 book for members. Fran also believed that the Society should get back with a university press, for distribution and prestige purposes. She recommended that I see Trudy McMurrin, the new director of SMU Press, since most of the TFS books were at SMU Press.

I met Trudy at the TFS meeting in Huntsville that Easter. She was agreeable, positive, up-beat all the way, and as excited as I was about the folk art book, which I meant to have to members for 1984. I told Trudy that I had the manuscripts and illustrations ready, and she told me that SMU had no other books in press at the time and that she could get it out in six months. We struck a deal that would be put in writing as soon as I got back to the office.

This move to SMU Press began as a happy reunion. The Society had been with SMU Press and Allen Maxwell and Margaret

Hartley from 1949 to 1966, and members looked at this venture as a natural homecoming. The honeymoon, however, was soon over.

The publication process began to break down immediately. I sent the manuscript with illustrations to SMU Press in May. I had no idea what was happening there, but throughout that summer I was continually assured that layout and typesetting were under way. At the end of September not one type had been set. This battle went on for well over a year. I was told that the books would be ready by the first of the 1985, then by the Easter meeting at the latest. I naively mailed SMU the shipping labels in March, to no avail. I will not bore the reader with calumnies that the editor and publisher exchanged over that period. Suffice it to say, that I at one time was considering pulling the book in the middle of production.

Folk Art in Texas (PTFS 44), which was supposed to have been the members' book in 1984, was finally mailed in August of 1985.

Folk Art was a beautiful book, all and more than I expected it to be. And the Society paid the unbelievable amount of $20,000 toward its cost of production. But the ultimate cost to SMU Press was $44,148.18! for 3,500 books printed by Claude Smithhart of Lufkin (Texas) Printing Company. When I received the bill for that amount I nearly suffered a stroke, but I had earlier pledged the $20,000, and I never intended to pay more. And the Society never did.

Folk Art was a coffee-table book and retailed for $35.00.

In the November elections the Republican Reagan-Bush ticket swept forty-nine states in its victory over the Democratic Mondale-Ferraro ticket.

1985

Joe S. Graham

President 1984–85 at Abilene

Professor of Sociology at Texas A&M University at Kingsville, curator of John E. Conner Museum, formerly Folklorist in Residence at Institute of Texan Cultures, editor of *Hecho en Tejas* (PTFS 50)

Senator Ralph Yarborough joined the TFS in the Sixties and was a regular dues paying member for the next two decades. The Society would get a letter from him every year at dues time. He would always mention the upcoming meeting and send regrets that he could not attend. Then he would add a handwritten note about our last publication or some detail of the Society to show that he was concerned and keeping up. I cherish those notes and his interest in the Society, which went back to the Dobie days.

Joe Graham of Texas A&M presided at the Abilene meeting, April 4–6, 1985. Joe was raised on a ranch in the Big Bend, and he could write about Mexican culture with knowledge, sympathy, and a personal understanding. He served as Folklorist in Residence at the Institute of Texan Cultures before he became a professor at A&M. We met at the Kiva Inn, and the meeting was sponsored by the Abilene Cultural Affairs Council, the Texas Commission on the Arts, and the National Endowment of the Arts, an imposing trio. Lawrence and Sonja Clayton were the local arrangers.

At the paper session Sonja Clayton introduced her west Texas cowboy friends: Cliff Teinert, the Ledbetter and Peacock families, and the famous Watkins Reynolds Matthews of Lambshead. Betty

Casey gave a paper entitled "Dance Across Texas" and presented the Betty Casey western dancers in a routine that would have looked good in *Oklahoma!* The banquet speaker for the Abilene meeting was John Erickson of Perryton reading from his Hank the Cowdog books. He made a hilarious presentation, and I have been a Hank the Cowdog fan ever since.

The editor was still battling with the director of SMU Press, this time on editing *Sonovagun Stew: A Folklore Miscellany* (PTFS 46–1985). To complicate matters, *Folk Art*, the book for 1984, was still in press.

The editing policy for miscellanies from Frank Dobie through Mody Boatright and Wilson Hudson to the present editor has always been liberal. We all believed that the individual writers of essays knew what they wanted to say and how they wanted to say it, and we pretty well left their papers alone. We did regularize spelling, punctuation, grammar, and documentation, and we had no quarrel with people of the press who caught mechanical errors that we had overlooked. But none of us wanted an editor who did such corrections as changing sentence structure so that the writing would "sound better." We were able to clear the *Sonovagun Stew* editing hurdle with only a little blood spilled.

I had begun sending edited manuscripts for *Sonovagun Stew* to the press in January so that they could edit and put them on the computer as each came in. The press had all manuscripts in April and shipped the book nine months later, in December. Claude Smithhart of Lufkin Printing ran two thousand copies at $8.43 each, or $17,573.91 total. I wrote Trudy McMurrin on December 13, 1985, that I liked the book and that she had done a fine job, which she had, but what a battle!

The TFS office also experienced secretarial problems again in 1985. Marlene Adams had the temerity to get pregnant and give birth during her Society tenure. She was babying from January to March, during which time I survived with student help that almost cratered the bookkeeping. Marlene returned in April, got the books in order, wrote a how-to plan for TFS secretaries, then moved to California with her husband in August. Carrol Daniels, bless her heart! came in that fall and saved the Society from complete collapse.

In the February 5, 1985, newsletter the editor announced naively that the book for 1987 would be the history of the TFS—in one volume! Problems arose. Just six months later the editor began the July 8, 1985, newsletter: "This proposed Texas Folklore Society history volume started off simply enough; we were going to publish the TFS programs in order to have them down in the records. Then we began to add lists of past officers and presidents. Then somebody suggested people pictures and program covers, and biographies and reminiscences, and we now have in the planning stage a major publication whose purpose is to bring together in *one volume* (editor's italics) all of the Society's relevant material." I wrote five paragraphs of planning for that one-volume TFS history. Little did I know!

Trudy McMurrin, Director of SMU Press from 1983 to 1986

1986

Melvin R. Mason
President 1985–86 at Jefferson
Professor of English for forty-five years in public schools, colleges, and universities, retired from Sam Houston State University, author and documentarist of *Martha Mitchell of Possum Walk Road: Texas Quiltmaker*

This was the year of the Texas Sesquicentennial. Archie McDonald, Hazel, and I toured South Australia giving talks about Texas history and folklore. This was South Australia's Sesquicentennial also. I was home from Australia about a month before I went to the University of Harbin, China, to talk about teaching English to Chinese students. And I had just gotten back from England on the Thursday of the TFS meeting. This was a year of travel.

From the January 22, 1986, newsletter, here is the reason that as far back as 1986 this TFS history began to get unwieldy:

"I just got back from two full days at the Barker Center going through the Society's files. Fascinating! A mighty amount of energy has been poured into this outfit since 1909, some blood spilled, some laurels won, but always a love of the lore and pleasure in the pursuit. I am presently just getting all the records in order, year by year: officers, minutes of meetings (with Dobie cussing somebody who spoke too long and laboriously), programs, publications (with some teeth-grinding battles between editors and publishers), financial statements. I found some interesting mentionables, such as a Society resolution against state legislation banning state employment to members of the N.A.A.C.P. I chanced upon interesting unmentionables, such as the case of one now venerable and sainted lady who was discussed as the other woman in an inter-Society divorce case and was at the time in hot pursuit of another of the Society's patriarchs."

The members' book for 1986 was Betty Casey's *Dance Across Texas* (ExB 19). Betty lived in Kerrville, taught dancing, and wrote books about dancing. *Dance Across Texas* contained the history of dancing in Texas and instructions for square dancing and line dancing, popular pastimes in the best honky-tonks in Texas in 1986. The Urban Cowboy was alive and well in Texas, as well as in New York and London. The University of Texas Press produced *Dance Across Texas*, and Charles Shaw did a beautiful dust jacket of a bunch of folks dancing the "Cotton-Eyed Joe."

Folk Art in Texas won the 1985 Book of the Year Award (as had *Singin' Texas* in 1984), presented by the San Antonio Conservation Society.

Trudi McMurrin wrote (April 7, 1986) that she was leaving SMU and going back west, to Utah, I think. We parted amicably enough. I wrote her: "Yeah, we've had rocky times but you got out two books [*Folk Art* and *Sonovagun Stew*] that I'm very proud of, and I thank you for that" (April 14, 1986). On July 2, SMU announced the appointment of Keith Gregory, formerly director of TCU Press, as the new director of SMU press. Keith wrote me on August 25, telling about his choice of my old friend Suzanne Comer of the University of Texas Press as his Senior Editor. He also had hired the award-winning Barbara and Fred Whitehead of Austin as book designers. It was a whole new ballgame, and this editor was happy.

With Sarah Greene, publisher-editor of *The Gilmer Mirror*, as hostess and local arranger, the Society met in historic Jefferson, Texas, March 27–29, 1986. Fortunately, we all arrived on the same Easter date. In the January 22, 1986, newsletter, we misannounced the meeting date as being in April instead of March. Another mailing and a correction followed hard upon its heels, and as far as I know, nobody showed up for TFS in April. Melvin Mason of Huntsville was the president that year. Melvin was a professor of English at Sam Houston State University at the time and deep into the study of old-time camp meetings and gospel singings. Officers and dignitaries of the 1986 meeting stayed at the Excelsior House, members elsewhere. All of the sessions were held in the Old Opera House.

Highlights of the meeting were Joyce Roach's "A High Toned Woman," a paper which has set the definition and standard for high-toned women everywhere ever since—just as Jim Lee set the definitions for "Mothers and Others" in an earlier paper. At the Friday night banquet Wyatt Moore of Carnack on Caddo Lake talked about his life on the big lake and building the Texas planked pirogue, which I have ever since threatened to do.

Lowlights! In 1986 the Society was under the governance of a Board of Directors and Councilors, one of whose duties was to recommend candidates for Society offices, particularly the office of vice president-program chairmen. The Board did this not to maintain an "old buddy" system but to be sure that those people who contributed to the welfare and running of the Society were not overlooked. Thus the Board had a list of two or three members whom they decided should be nominated down the line. The chain of communication and decision broke down at the Jefferson business meeting. The embarrassing result was that two candidates were in the running for the vice presidency, the most important position. Factions and considerable ill will were generated by that political gaffe. The hard and hurt feelings took several years to get over.

A review of 1985's *Sonovagun Stew* in *True West* (November 1986) criticized the book because it was not about cooking and recipes. We had the same response earlier to *Paisanos*, which the reviewer thought was a book about birds, and *T for Texas*, which some thought was about country music. Good titles are hard to come by.

To remind you of the 1986 that was. . . . My generation remembers the exact moment of hearing about Pearl Harbor and John Kennedy's assassination. As vividly in my memory is the moment I learned of the Challenger disaster—and the pictures of the shuttle blowing apart. The Challenger tragedy was almost too much for the American people; several years would pass before we regained the stomach necessary for space exploration. We are still learning and suffering from the meltdown at Chernobyl. Did we learn anything from revelations of the Iran-Contra scandal, when the U. S. secretly sold arms to its enemy

Iran and secretly sent the proceeds to help the rebels in Nicaragua? On a brighter note, Larry McMurtry won the Pulitzer for *Lonesome Dove*.

Howard Wilcox (–1987), left, and Leroy Brown (1910–1997), below, Society benefactors

1987

Jim Harris
President 1986–87 at Galveston
Teaches English at New Mexico Junior College in Hobbs, honored as a New Mexico Eminent Scholar, writes poetry, fiction, and newspaper columns, edited *Features and Fillers* (PTFS 56–1999)

The Texas Folklore Society went to Galveston in 1987. We wore white flannel trousers and walked along the beach and heard the mermaids singing each to each. And they sang to us, as did Jim Harris, the poet-president at the 1987 meeting.

—for the members
On down the coast last month
they met on South Padre
exhuberant over the coming of spring
faces full of the joys of self singing
bodies as nimble as the loose suits that confined them.

On the surface
as one thin layer of wet sand
it seems we would be their opposites
at this northern end of the Texas coast:
mostly older with a new spring,
suits fitting tighter than last year
faces celebrating traditions rooted
if not in the deep past, at least
tied to patience and practice,

moving a little slower in our boots
backs bent under the weight of a guitar,
voices hoarse from a Lomax song
or a Dobie tale
or a Boatright joke.

But we are also kids on the beach
revelers of the present too;
the tides that tie gulls to this string of watery lands
bind southern and northern islands,
coastal plains and seashore dunes, and
our desires to theirs:

to know the shape of this landscape
to have a knowledge and experience of our own place
to be rich
with a hunger for the genuine and worthy.

President Jim and Mary Harris made a vacation of his year's presidency; they visited Galveston three times, being wined and dined by the convention bureau, given champagne in free hotel rooms, and taken on grand tours of the city. They deserved the attention. Jim is the Society's token New Mexican, an English teacher at New Mexico Junior College in Hobbs. He is also a short story writer and a newspaper columnist, and I am proud to say, one of my former folklore students.

We met at the Key Largo Hotel, a very ritzy establishment in spite of the tackiness of their lounge band competing with our hootenanny. We had a good set of papers, as usual. Memorably, Al Lowman continued his "Elephant Ears" saga, and Ken Davis added a chapter to his Bell County tales. Lowman's story of the REA bringing in electricity in the 1940s and turning on the Christmas lights at his house left few dry eyes. The same might be said for Davis's tale of a wake in Bell County during which the corpse understandably created a clear-the-house panic with a midnight scream. For the Friday night banquet President Harris brought the New Mexico novelist, Rudy Anaya, who spoke of his use of Hispanic folkways in his fiction.

PTFS 47 for 1987 was a traditional miscellany entitled *Hoein' the Short Rows,* which had as little to do with agricultural practices as *Sonovagun Stew* had with home cooking. This volume was dedicated to Martha Emmons, the grande dame of the Society, who had been a contributing member for sixty-four years, since 1924, and had been TFS president twice. Miss Martha had retired from teaching at Baylor University but was still working in the university library.

Hoein' was Suzanne Comer's first TFS book for SMU Press. The manuscript got to her by the first of the 1987 and after a few bumps and grinds she had it in the hands of members in January 1988. It did not get out when it was supposed to, but we had no battles nor personal conflicts, which was a welcome relief. She printed 2,038 copies for $13,236, about four thousand dollars less than the previous *Sonavagun Stew*.

Howard Wilcox, a Beaumont pathologist and friend of the Society, had gifted the Society with checks of denominations from the hundreds to the thousands since 1985. They were checks that he had received for services rendered that he deemed as charitable, so he extended the charity to the Society. This was a time of rising interest rates. Thus, the $10,000-plus that he cast upon TFS waters in 1986 and 1987 increased annually and has been a blessing to the Society ever since. In June, 1987, Howard endorsed to the Society three checks—$750, $500, and $1000—in addition to a box of pecans. On August 17, 1987, Howard Wilcox went to bed and died peacefully in his sleep, the ultimate reward for his many good deeds.

The Society's balance at the end of 1987 was $88,215.23.

I certainly have no trouble remembering 1987; that was the year the university remodeled the Rusk Building, in which the Texas Folklore Society offices reside. The Rusk Building is the second oldest on the campus. We had been remodeled about ten years before, and it had thrown the Society's business into confusion for a few months. The administration had tried to move me and the TFS office then, but I dragged my feet and hid out in a dungeon room under the stairs until they finished. This time I got a letter from the vice president saying the Society had to move to new offices. The day I got it I dashed back to my office and drew a master expansion plan which took in the room next to the TFS office and two large storerooms. I ran the plan over to SFA President William Johnson, asked him to include it in the new plans, and he agreed. The presidents of SFA have always been supportive of the Society. So the office suffered for several months, I hid out in the dungeon again and battled a disagreeable construction foreman, but eventually we got back into an office that is still the largest and grandest on the campus, well suited to the exalted status of the Texas Folklore Society.

In addition to the confusion of remodeling, the Society bought a computer in the spring of 1987. It had a hard mouth and a rough gait, but Carrol and I finally arrived at a time where we could use it with some control and comfort. The learning experience, however, was (is!) traumatic.

Suzanne Comer (1945–1990), Senior Editor of SMU Press from 1985 to 1989

1988

Lou Halsell Rodenberger
President 1987–88 at Lubbock
Professor Emeritus of English at McMurry University in Abilene, a Texas Voices Humanities Scholar, published essays on rural schoolteacher parents, Texas women writers, southwestern writers, *Her Work: Stories by Texas Women*, and co-edited *Texas Women Writers: A Tradition of Their Own*

George Bush became president in 1988, and a Pan Am 747 was blown out of the air over Lockerbie, Scotland, killing all aboard.

But if you are a brass-collared Democrat who refuses to remember that George Bush was elected that year, you will remember that when we met in Lubbock that Easter the weather turned upside down. Ken Davis remembers that "we had snow, sleet, rain, hail" and then on Saturday afternoon we had a Panhandle spring day. Ken and Jeri Tanner arranged that meeting, and Lou Rodenberger was the president. Lou had been a professor of Engish at A&M before she moved to McMurry College in Abilene. She is a prolific writer, specializing in women's studies and much influenced by her parents' lives as rural school teachers. The Society met at Lubbock's Holiday Inn and Convention Center, and everybody paid proper respects to Buddy Holly at his statue nearby.

We also paid proper respects to Martha Emmons and her sixty-four years as a member and moral guide in the Society. This meeting was dedicated to Martha, who was feted with a suite and bouquets of flowers. One session—composed of Jim Byrd, Jim Lee, and the editor—was devoted to roasting and toasting the grande dame of the TFS. In his more kindly remarks, Jim Byrd said, "I'd be a heap mo' ignorant than I am without Martha. In the past 30 years, she made a Texan out of me [an Alabaman]. When I'm with her, which has been a lot, I forget I wasn't born and bred in the briar patch of East Texas."

We had full attendance at the Lubbock meeting, in spite of its being "way out there." Over three hundred attended the banquet, where Elmer Kelton gave his speech, "Fiction Writers Are Liars and Thieves," later published in *The Bounty of Texas* (PTFS 49–1990). As one of Texas' foremost fiction writers and Society supporters, Elmer discussed his use of history and folklore in his western novels: "We steal stories wherever we find them, disguise them, paint them up like car thieves in a chop shop, then present them as our own" (*Bounty of Texas,* 51).

At the business meeting the Society voted to have five directors and five councilors who would serve three-year terms. Traditionally the president became a director at the end of his or her term. This regularized the number of directors and councilors, which over the years had varied.

The International Congress on Anthropological and Ethnological Sciences met at Zagreb, Yugoslavia, on July 24–31, 1988. Their library of science publications included four PTFSs: *Built in Texas, Folk Art in Texas, Legendary Ladies of Texas,* and *Singin' Texas.*

Texas Toys and Games had been in the making for over a year in 1988, but it was still not ready to go to press. Toys and games were still coming in from contributors, and there were gaps to be filled and pictures to be taken. Fortunately, John O. West of El Paso had come out in 1988 with his *Mexican-American Folklore* (ExB 20–1988), published by August House in Little Rock. *Mexican-American Folklore* fitted Society criteria of being a member's book about a significant field of folklore. It was one of the richest extra books the Society has ever used.

Seventieth Annual Meeting of the Texas Folklore Society ★★ Jefferson
March 27, 28 & 29 in the Texas Sesquicentennial Year, 1986

1989

Sarah L. Greene
President 1988–89 at Uvalde
Owner, publisher, and editor of *The Gilmer Mirror*, Director of Gilmer National Bank, Woman of Courage Award, Woman of the Year, Headliner of the Year, Anson Jones Award, among her honors

Texas Toys and Games (PTFS 48–1989) did not come out in 1989. Members finally received their book in late February of 1990. Refreshing my memory about the book's gestation, I quote the following history from the *TT&G* preface:

"Lee Haile is responsible for its conception. In 1982—on Saturday, April 10, at 11:00 A.M., to be exact—at the Sunday House in Fredericksburg, Lee, then a student of Texas A&M, presented a paper with the most unacademic of titles, "Seven Toys We Made for Free." He spun, whirled, bounced and talked about his toys for his allotted twenty minutes and instructed and delighted all present. He expanded his talk and discussed homemade toys again in the spring of 1984 for the Texas State Historical Association. Then in 1985 when I started filling in folk topics for the *Handbook of Texas*, getting Lee to do the entry on "Folk Toys" was a natural conclusion.

"At the same time that I was filling the Texas folk toys entry for the *Handbook*, I was looking for someone to do the companion entry on "Folk Games." Martha Hartzog of the Alta Vista Productions in Austin volunteered for that topic, and I had the beginning of *Texas Toys and Games*. I didn't consider the two for a

PTFS though, even after Suzanne Comer, then with the University of Texas Press, said that she was interested in seeing a book on Texas toys and games.

"Then in the July 1986 newsletter I asked for suggestions for special PTFS topics, and Janette Swadley wrote that she and Don and Ben Capps, during a deliberation over libations, had decided that we should have a volume on toys and games. She very generously volunteered Ben's services, and [*Texas Toys and Games*] was under way."

Toys and games turned out to be an exciting but demanding project. I had a lot of fun collecting toys for illustrations. Researching, building, and playing with the toys and games brought back many memories. Over a decade later those toys are still scattered about the TFS office, and periodically I am called upon to talk about Texas toys and games to kids and grownups. The book itself sold well from the beginning, and the Society brought out a second printing in 1997.

But this was the third SMU Press book running that did not make it to members on time. In the "January" newsletter the editor wrote the following on February 14, 1990:

"My ultimate dread as editor of the Society's annual publications is to have to mail out the February meeting invitation-newsletter before the book for the previous year is with the members. It has happened a couple of times before. It has happened again. The Society's relationship with SMU Press, as many years as it has endured, is, I now believe, cursed. The problems began in the Fifties. We went our separate ways finally, only to come together again, but the curse remains. *Texas Toys and Games* text was at the Press in March of '89 with the understanding that the book would be out in October or early November. This time came, was changed to November 31, then slated for December 15. A sample book showed up around that date but was so flawed that it had to be returned to the maker, to be in the hands of the members by January 15, 1990! An inquiry after that date revealed the book was trapped in a Mexican standoff between the publisher and the printer about who would pay for corrections. That was finally resolved and the book was promised on February 15, 1990! Who knows? I explain this to the newer members of the Society.

Long-time members recognize and sympathize with the problems of publication. So, look for *Texas Toys and Games* when you see it coming. I hope it is in your lifetime, and mine."

Texas Toys and Games was finally mailed to members in late February 1990. We ran two thousand copies for $15,366. The market price was $24.95 for hardback and $19.95 for paperback. *TT&G*, attractively laid out by Barbara Whitehead, sold well from its beginning.

In 1990, the Society moved its publication program from SMU Press to the University of North Texas Press under the new directorship of Fran Vick, formerly our publisher with E-Heart Press. No hard feelings were involved. Suzanne Comer did what she could with SMU's publication program. Tragically that sweet, dear girl died in the summer of 1990 with cancer.

The Society had concerns other than *TT&G* in 1989. We had our seventy-third annual meeting at the Holiday Inn in Uvalde on March 23–25. The meeting was presided over by Sarah Greene, owner-publisher-editor of *The Gilmer Mirror* and honored above all women in East Texas journalism. The meeting was hosted by Lora B. and Roger Garrison of Uvalde, who took members on John Nance Garner tours and ranch tours. We witnessed a formando of the remuda at the Chaparrosa Ranch. Vaqueros popped their lariats and whips, and the horses accomodatingly backed up to a stretched rope and stood there respectfully waiting to be bridled. I am still amazed. The formando certainly beats roping horses out of a lariat corral.

The banquet entertainment was a film about the bank robbing Newton Brothers of Uvalde, who had served their time and were now sitting around town being famous.

The Society also honored a special guest, Sarah Payne Foxworth, the daughter of TFS founder Leonidas W. Payne. Sarah and the Texas Folklore Society were born within days of each other, so we celebrated the eightieth anniversary of both. Leonidas missed the Dallas founding meeting in 1909 in the expectation of the birth of Sarah, who was a week late. Sarah came to the Uvalde meeting with book in hand, having worked with Hansen Alexander in the writing and publishing of the biography of her father, *Rare Integrity: A Portrait of L. W. Payne, Jr.*, by Wind River Press, Austin.

Carrol Daniels retired as this office's secretary in the spring of 1989. The usual panic ensued before Mrs. Carolyn Fiedler Satterwhite signed on as secretary. Carolyn quickly and efficiently became the assistant editor of publications and the manager of the Society's office.

The Society closed out the decade of the Eighties with a balance of $112,655.25! Even though we were paying inflationary prices in our publishing program, we were receiving inflationary interest on our savings and investments. But I am continually amazed by the Society's solvency.

In early June of that year I was standing by my hotel window looking down on a misty street in Innsbruck when I heard the news of the Tiananmen Square massacre. I ached in disappointment. The China I had visited three years earlier had been moving with such optimism toward a freer and more open social, political, and economic plateau than China had known in decades. Or so I thought and so it appeared. But the dark forces that have always underlain political power bases, triumphed again. This was 1989's tragedy—along with the *Exxon Valdez* oil spill in Prince William Sound, Alaska, where the *Pride of Valdez* had once seined those cold clear waters for salmon.

Carrol Daniels, office secretary from 1985 to 1989

Meetings and Publications of the Texas Folklore Society 1979 to 1989

Sixty-third annual meeting, held at Waco, April 12–14, 1979, at the Sheraton Inn. Hosted by Baylor University.

Officers

President: James M. Day, El Paso

Vice-President: Robert J. Duncan, Mesquite

Secretary-Editor: Francis E. Abernethy, Nacogdoches

Treasurer: Edwin W. Gaston, Jr., Nacogdoches

Directors: Martha Emmons, Waco; Ernest Speck, Alpine; Geoffrey Grimes, Dallas; Ernestine Sewell, Arlington; Joyce Roach, Keller

Councilors: Joe Graham, Alpine; Peter Stephan, Salt Lake City, Utah; Lawrence Clayton, Abilene; Sylvia Grider, College Station; Sarah Greene, Gilmer; Charles Linck, Commerce; Jim Harris, Hobbs, New Mexico; Archie McDonald, Nacogdoches

Program Chairman: Robert J. Duncan, Mesquite

Local arrangements: Linda K. Walker (Chairperson), Margaret Davis, Patricia Howard, J.R. LeMaster, English Department Teaching Assistants, Sigma Tau Delta

Program

Thursday: Registration, Cruise on The Brazos Queen, Hootenanny.

Friday, first session:

Presiding: James W. Byrd, Commerce

"Legends in Their Own Times: The Cowboy Cheerleaders," James Ward Lee, Denton

"Rock Art of the Big Bend," Miriam A. Lowrance, Alpine

"The Big Bird Flap," Jan Seale, Edinburg

Second session:

Presiding: George D. Hendricks, Denton

"Night Horse Nightmare," Paul Patterson, Crane

"Pardon Me, Governor Ferguson," Maisie Paulissen, Houston

"Things That Fall Down Between the Cracks of Texas History," June R. Welch, Dallas

Third session:

Presiding: Charles B. Martin, Denton

"Hands Around the World: Norway," Geoffrey A. Grimes, Dallas

"A Key of Golden—A Happy Life," Mrs. John Q. Anderson, Ruston, La.

"The Day of the Dead in Northern Mexico," John O. West, El Paso

Fourth session:

Presiding: Sylvia Grider, College Station

Student Paper Contest Winner—Undergraduate

Student Paper Contest Winner—Graduate

"Busing the Bankers—1967 Style," William N. Stokes, Jr., Lake Dallas

"Mexican-American Folk Housing," Joe S. Graham, San Antonio

Banquet singers: The Spiritual Singers of Antioch Baptist Church

Saturday, fifth session:

Presiding: Martha Emmons, Waco

"Animal Metaphors and Verbal Abuse: A Study of Social Relations and Values Among German-Speaking Farmers on Cypress Creek, Kerr County, Texas," Glen E. Lich, San Marcos
"Your Soul to the Devil, or Curses! The Irish Are at It Again," Ann Miller, Waco
"More Crude from the Permian Basin," Jim Harris, Hobbs, New Mexico
Sixth session:
Presiding: Jeri Tanner, Lubbock
"Reestablishing the Oral Lore of the Hunting Archer," Lawrence Clayton, Abilene
"Rural Texas Reminiscences," Bill Porterfield, Dallas
"Scoops, FYI's and Cablese: Journalism and the Journalist as Folklore," Ernest B. Speck, Alpine
Business meeting

Built in Texas. PTFS XLII. Francis Edward Abernethy, editor. Waco: E-Heart Press, 1979.

CONTENTS

Sixty-fourth annual meeting, held at San Antonio, April 3–5, 1980, at the Institute of Texan Cultures.

Officers

President: Robert J. Duncan, McKinney

Vice-President: Lawrence Clayton, Abilene

Secretary-Editor: Francis E. Abernethy, Nacogdoches

Treasurer: Edwin W. Gaston, Jr., Nacogdoches

Directors: Geoffrey Grimes, DeSoto; Joyce Roach, Keller; Ernestine Sewell, Arlington; Joe Graham, Presidio; James M. Day, El Paso

Councilors: Claudia Ball, San Antonio; Sylvia Grider, College Station; Archie McDonald, Nacogdoches; Sarah Greene, Gilmer; Charles Linck, Commerce; Jim Harris, Hobbs, New Mexico

Program Chairman: Lawrence Clayton, Abilene

Local Arrangements: Claudia Ball, Jo Ann Andera, Joan Kete, Dorothy Taylor

Program

Thursday: Registration, Hootenanny

Friday, first session, Joe Graham, Presidio, presiding:

"The Origin and Originators of Pecos Bill," James M. Day, El Paso

"Texas's Country School Teachers: Living Proof of a Legend," Lou Rodenberger, College Station

"Architectural and Decorative Uses of Petrified Wood," Sylvia Ann Grider, College Station

Second session, Glen E. Lich, New Orleans, Louisiana, presiding:

"Beyond the Limpopoma," Jeri Tanner, Lubbock

"The National Folklore festival in Coban, Guatemala," Charles B. Martin, Denton

"An Invitation from 'The Land of Eternal Spring': The Fourth Annual Invitational Americas Studies Conference," Geoffrey Allan Grimes

Third session, Melvin Mason, Huntsville, presiding:

"Folk Shrines Along the Rio Bravo," John O. West, El Paso

"Folklorish Remnants of Peyote Ceremonialism," Ernestine Sewell, Arlington; Charles Linck, Commerce

"Pissing on the Elephant Ears & Other True Stories," Al Lowman, San Antonio

Fourth session, Jim Harris, Hobbs, New Mexico, presiding:

"God and the Garden," Ernest Speck, Alpine

"Funsies in the Courthouse," William N. Stokes, Jr., Lake Dallas

"Within the Walls: Texas Prison Folklore," Martha Anne Turner, Huntsville

Banquet speaker: Robert Flynn, San Antonio, "Growing up a Sullen Baptist; Blessed and Unreconciled"
Saturday, fifth session:
Presiding: Don Swadley, Arlington
"My Favorite Texan and Folklore," Mrs. John Q. Anderson, Ruston, Louisiana
"Dogs —AND Dogs," Palmer Olsen, Clifton
"A Place Against the Sky," Martha Emmons, Waco
Sixth session:
Presiding: James W. Byrd, Commerce
"Things That Fall Down Between the Cracks of Texas History," June Welch, Dallas
"A Texas Cowboy Down Under," Paul Patterson, Crane
"Preachers, Teachers, and Meddlers," James Ward Lee, Denton
Business meeting

Sixty-fifth annual meeting, held at Denton, April 16–18, 1981, at the Holiday Inn. Meeting hosted by North Texas State University.
Officers
President: Lawrence Clayton, Abilene
Vice-President: Charles Martin, Denton
Secretary-Editor: Francis E. Abernethy, Nacogdoches
Treasurer: Edwin W. Gaston, Nacogdoches
Directors: Joyce Roach, Keller; Ernestine Sewell, Arlington; Joe Graham, College Station; James M. Day, El Paso; Robert J. Duncan, McKinney
Councilors: Archie McDonald, Nacogdoches Sarah Greene, Gilmer; Charles Linck, Commerce; Jim Harris, Hobbs, New Mexico; Joseph Jones, Austin; Al Lowman, San Antonio
Local arrangements: James Ward Lee, Gabe Antonatos, Peg Antonatos, Joyce Glover, John T. Smith, Beth White, Robert Hughes
Program
Thursday: Registration, Singing
Friday, First session, Stan Alexander, Nacogdoches, presiding:
Welcome: Sam H. Henderson, Denton
"Cuttin' Beddin," Paul Patterson, Crane
"The Totems of the Haida Indians of the Alaska Panhandle," Dorys C. Grover, Commerce
"On the Marking of Blind Lemon Jefferson's Grave," James L. Baird, Denton
Second session, Claudia Ball, San Antonio, presiding:
"When Elephant Ears Last in the Dooryard Proliferated: Further Notes on the Paragglutination and Psycho-Historical Implications of the Diverse Social and Cultural Phenomena Observed in Staples and Northern Guadalupe County, Texas, and Reflected in the Oral Tradition," Al Lowman, San Antonio
"Frank Norfleet: Monte Cristo of the High Plains," William N. Stokes, Lake Dallas
"The Limberjack: A Traditional American Dancing Doll," Sylvia Grider, College Station
Third session, Joyce Roach, Keller, presiding:

"The Automatic 'Howdy': Folk Communication Today," James W. Byrd, Commerce
"A Key of Golden—A Happy Life, Part II," Loraine Anderson, Ruston, Louisiana
Fourth session, Martha Emmons, Waco, presiding:
"When You Call Me That, Smile," F. E. Abernethy, Nacogdoches
"Equines and Others," Ernest Speck, Alpine
Banquet welcome: Jim B. Pearson, NTSU
Music: Voices of Praise, Denton
Fifth session, John O. West, El Paso, presiding:
"Mexican-American Folk Foods: Confluence of Cultures," Joe S. Graham, College Station
"Hands Around the World: Folk Motifs of Japan," Diane Musha, Carrollton
Sixth session, Elmer Kelton, San Angelo, presiding:
"Monument: Folklife of a Frontier Community," Jim Harris, Hobbs, New Mexico
"Possible Origins of the Appalachian Clog Dance," Jerry Duke, San Francisco, California
Report on the TFS Visit to Guatemala, Geoffrey L. Grimes, Dallas
Business meeting.

Legendary Ladies of Texas. PTFS XLIII. Francis Edward Abernethy, editor. Dallas, E-Heart Press, 1981.

CONTENTS

Sixty-sixth annual meeting, held at Fredericksburg, April 8–10, 1982, at the Sunday House Motel.

Officers

President: Charles Martin, Denton

Vice-President: Sylvia Grider, College Station

Secretary-Editor: F.E. Abernethy, Nacogdoches

Treasurer: Edwin W. Gaston, Nacogdoches

Directors: Joe Graham, College Station; James M. Day, El Paso; Robert J. Duncan, McKinney; Lawrence Clayton, Abilene; Ed Offield, Dallas

Councilors: Charles Linck, Commerce; Jim Harris, Hobbs, New Mexico; Joseph Jones, Austin; Al Lowman, San Marcos; Claudia Ball, San Antonio; Bill Stokes, Dallas

Local Arrangements: Mary Elizabeth Nye, J.B. Hutchinson

Program

Thursday: Registration, Singing

Friday, first session, Joe Graham, Texas A&M, presiding:

"The Rural Mailbox as Folk Art, With Stories of the Carriers," Ernestine Sewell, UT at Arlington

"Forty-Two Baptist Kids and Three Baptist Deacons: The Saga of a 'Churching,'" William N. Stokes, Jr., Dallas

"Singing Cowboys and Others from 'B' Westerns," Archie McDonald, Nacogdoches

Second session, John West, El Paso, presiding:

"A Comparison of the Songs of the American Cowboy and the Argentine Gaucho," Lawrence Clayton and Rosa Chazarreta, Hardin-Simmons University

"The Universality of Folk Lyrics," Connie Ricci, Rochester Public Schools

"All I Know About America Is What I See in the Commercials," B.W. Aston, Hardin-Simmons University

Third session, James Day, El Paso, presiding:

"Martha Mitchell of Possum Walk Road: Artist with Needle and Brush," Melvin Mason, Huntsville, with the assistance of John Westen McCoy (Photography) and Jan Cole (music)

"It All Wound Up in Bales," Ernest Speck, Sul Ross State University
"Blood on the Elephant Ears: Tales of Mayhem, Manslaughter, and Murder," Al Lowman, Institute of Texan Cultures
Fourth session, Jack Duncan, McKinney, presiding:
"'Can You Handle Them Ol' Big Boys?' Discipline in Texas Rural Schools," Lou Rodenberger, Blinn College
"Run to Win: A Southwestern Racetrack Folk Profile," Suzy Schoener, Texas A&M
"The Structure and Evolution of American Fiddle Tunes," Gene and Marynell Young, Texas A&M
Banquet welcome: Charles Martin
Guest of the Society: Wayland D. Hand
Dance: Jim Hartmann's Pehl's Old Time Band
Saturday, fifth session, Charles Rodenberger, Texas A&M, presiding:
"Religious Shenanigans," Palmer Olsen, Clifton
"The French Harp in Texas," Mike Licht, University of Texas
"The Rise of Cowboy Folklore," Jim McNutt, University of Texas
Sixth session, Charles Linck, Commerce, presiding:
"El Pachuco Nuevo: Macho? Si! Malo? No!," R.L. Cowser, Jr., Wharton County Junior College
"Seven Toys We Made for Free," Lee Haile, Texas A&M
"The Old Time Cowboy Inside Out," Paul Patterson, Crane
Business meeting

T for Texas: A State Full of Folklore. PTFS XLIV. Francis E. Abernethy, editor. Dallas: E-Heart Press, 1982.

CONTENTS

Sixty-seventh annual meeting, held at College Station, March 31–April 2, 1983, jointly with the Texas A&M University Friends of the Library, at the Ramada Inn.

Officers

President: Sylvia Grider, College Station

Vice-President: Charles Linck, Commerce

Secretary-Editor: Francis E. Abernethy, Nacogdoches

Treasurer: Edwin W. Gaston, Nacogdoches

Directors: Jack Duncan, McKinney; Lawrence Clayton, Abilene; Ed Offield, Dallas; Charles Martin, Denton; Jim Harris, Hobbs, New Mexico

Councilors: Joseph Jones, Austin; Al Lowman, San Antonio; Claudia Ball, San Antonio; Bill Stokes, Dallas; Lou Rodenberger, Abilene; Melvin Mason, Huntsville

Local Arrangements: Dawn Cox, Don Dyal, Joe Graham, Evelyn King, David Mellor, Suzy Schoener, Gene and Marynell Young

Program

Thursday: Registration, Hootenanny, Film: Musica Hispanica, Texas Institute of Cultures, presented by Jim McNutt

Friday, first session:

Welcome, Sylvia Grider, College Station

Presiding: Sarah Greene, Gilmer

"Please Drink the Water," Don Swadley, Arlington

"From Castle to Castle," Mary Nye, Dallas

"The Long Arm of the Law," Martha Emmons, Waco

"Heaven," Jim Lee, Denton

Second Session:

Presiding: Thomas Linton, College Station

"Old Army Went to Hell in 1958: Aggie War Stories from the Corps of Cadets," Joe Graham, College Station
"Bottle Caps, Paper Dolls, and Diverse Things," Loraine Anderson, Ruston, LA
"A Super Reality," Faye Leeper, Midland
"Aggie Incredibles," Palmer Olsen, Clifton
Third session:
Presiding: Jim McNutt, San Antonio
"Bill Barton, Saddlemaker," Lawrence Clayton, Abilene
"Custer's Folly," Jessie McGaw, Houston
"Texas Cockers and Their Lingo," James Day, El Paso
"Twobits, Fourbits, or High School Cheerleading as a Lay Folk Ritual," Ernest Speck, Alpine
Fourth session:
Presiding: Jim Byrd, Commerce
"A High Toned Woman," Joyce Roach, Keller
"Texas Breeze—Kansas Cyclone—Carrie Nation," Bill Stokes, Dallas
"Mildew on the Elephant Ears," Al Lowman, San Antonio
"Five Hundred Roy Bedichek Letters—Folklorists Will Revel in Them," William A. Owens, Nyack, NY
Banquet speaker: John Graves
Fifth session:
Presiding: Paul Patterson, Crane
"Leave off and Add to: Transmission of Folk Tradition Through Quilts," Melvin Mason and Martha Mitchell, Huntsville
"The Great Hawaiian Jubilee: The Making of a Multi-Ethnic Folk Festival," Charles Martin, Denton
"Portrayal or Betrayal: The Legacy of the Buffalo Soldier in Art," Ray Willmuth, Fort Worth
"Let Me Tell You About a Song," Charles Townsend, Canyon
Sixth session, Frances Speck, Alpine, presiding.
"Old Copper Mining Towns in Arizona: From Rags to Riches to Rags," Don Walker, Lubbock
"A Texas Size Flea Market," Jack Duncan, McKinney
"You'll Always get Your Reward: Humor from the Copy Machine, Jim Harris, Hobbs, New Mexico
"Folk Grave Decoration Along the Rio Grande," John O. West, El Paso
Business session.

Sixty-eighth annual meeting, held at Huntsville, April 19–21, 1984, hosted by Sam Houston State University.
Officers
President: Charles Linck, Commerce
Vice-President: Joe Graham, Millican
Secretary-Editor: Francis E. Abernethy, Nacogdoches
Treasurer: Edwin W. Gaston, Nacogdoches
Directors: Lawrence Clayton, Abilene; Ed Offield, Dallas; Charles Martin, Denton; Jim Harris, Hobbs, New Mexico; Sylvia Grider, College Station
Councilors: Claudia Ball, San Antonio; Bill Stokes, Dallas; Lou Rodenberger,

Abilene; Melvin R. Mason, Huntsville; Frances Speck, Alpine; Art Hendrix, Commerce

Program

Thursday: Registration, President's Wine and Cheese/Autograph Party, Hootenanny featuring Martha Emmons

Friday morning, session one:

Presiding: Jim McNutt, San Antonio

"'The Cowboy's Christmas Ball': The Historicity of a Cowboy Ballad," Connie Ricci, Abilene

"The Snipe Hunt: A Folk Initiation Rite," Rhett Rushing, College Station

"Coyote: The Inverted Savior," Blake Burleson, Waco

Session two:

Presiding: Faye Leeper, Midland

"The Making of a Folklorist, Southern Style," John O. West, El Paso

"Mastering Schoolmastering in Forty (Years of) Easy Lessons," Paul Patterson, Crane

"Country School Teaching: More Than Just a Job," Lou Rodenberger, Abilene

Session three:

Presiding: Jack Duncan, McKinney

"Finding and Keeping Water in a Dry Country," Don Swadley, Arlington

"Firefly Lanterns and Floral Largesse," Loraine Anderson, Ruston, Louisiana

"Where the Home Fires Burn," Ernest Speck, Alpine

Session four:

Presiding: James Day, El Paso

"Hub Freeman, Blacksmith," Lawrence Clayton, Abilene

"Crazy People," Palmer Olsen, Clifton

"James Holcomb: Cockfighter," Jim Harris, Hobbs, New Mexico

Banquet, Charles Linck, presiding

Invocation: Melvin R. Mason, Huntsville

Welcome: Richard A. Cording, Dean, College of Arts and Sciences, SHSU

Introduction of speaker: Joe Graham

Address: "What Shall We Do with the Folk Arts?—Thoughts of a Native Daughter," Bess Lomax Hawes, Director, Folk Arts Program, National Endowment of the Arts, Washington, D.C.

Hootenanny

Saturday, session five:

Presiding: Sylvia Grider, College Station

"Folk Aesthetics," Joe Graham, Millican

"Alive and Well: Contemporary Folk Arts in Texas," Pat Jasper, Austin

"Yard Art," F.E. Abernethy, Nacogdoches

"A Memory of Love: The Textile Arts of Ava Johnson Cox," Constance Higdon, Austin

Session six:

Presiding: Pat Jasper, Austin

"From Bricks to Bricolage: Jose Varela, Figural Ceramicist," Suzanne Seriff, Austin

"People Don't Know the Comfort That Can Be in a Saddle: W.M. West, Saddlemaker," Jan Guy, Austin

"The Quilt and Its Maker: An Historical Approach," Beverly Crane, Dallas
"Stoney Knows How," Alan Governar, Dallas (film)
Business meeting, Charles Linck, presiding

Folk Art in Texas. PTFS XLV. Francis E. Abernethy, editor. Dallas, SMU Press, 1984

CONTENTS

Sixty-ninth annual meeting, held at Abilene, April 4–6, 1985, hosted by Hardin-Simmons University.

Officers
President: Joe Graham, Millican
Vice-President: Melvin R. Mason, Huntsville
Secretary-Editor: Francis E. Abernethy, Nacogdoches
Treasurer: Edwin W. Gaston, Nacogdoches

Directors: Charles Martin, Denton; Jim Harris, Hobbs, New Mexico; Sylvia Grider, College Station; Charles Linck, Commerce; Elmer Kelton, San Angelo

Councilors: Lou Rodenberger, Abilene; Frances Speck, Alpine; Art Hendrix, Commerce; Jim McNutt, San Antonio; Faye Leeper, Midland; Loraine Anderson, Ruston, Louisiana

Program

Thursday: Registration, Book Displays, Hootenanny

Friday morning (first session):

Presiding: Melvin R. Mason, Huntsville

"Waco's Winter of Discontent—William Cowper Brann (The Iconoclast)," William N. Stokes, Jr., Dallas

"The Unicorn in the Garden in Texas," Jim Byrd, Commerce

"A Sort of Double Meaning: Folklore and Bricolage in Gipson's 'Trail-Driving Rooster,'" Glen E. Lich, Kerrville

"The Biggest Bust in American Politics: Gleanings from American Presidential Politics from Washington to Ferraro," Archie P. McDonald, Nacogdoches

Second session:

Presiding: Connie Ricci, Abilene

"Printing the TFS Program at Cow Hill Press, with Milt McAfee, Art Hendrix," Charles Linck and Ernestine Sewell, Commerce

"Bucky, a No-nonsense Donkey with Wisdom of Solomon," Palmer H. Olsen, Clifton

"Dance Across Texas—Then and Now," Betty Casey, Kerrville

Third session:

Presiding: Art Hendrix, Commerce

"Dorothy Scarborough: Early Texas Folklorist," Sylvia Grider, Bryan

"Pueblos, Adobe, and the Socorro Mission," John O. West, El Paso

"A Key of Golden: Practical Jokes and Vagaries," Mrs. John Q. Anderson, Ruston, Louisiana

Fourth session:

Presiding: Sarah L. Greene, Gilmer

"The Rules of Cockfighting," Jim Harris, Hobbs, New Mexico

"Tales Grandpa Told," Ernest B. Speck, Alpine

"The Peacock Brothers: Modern but Traditional Cowboys," Sonja Irwin Clayton, Abilene

Dinner, Joe Graham, presiding

Speaker: John Erickson, Perryton

Co-hosted by Taylor County Historical Commission

Fifth session:

Presiding: Priscilla Althaus, Huntsville

"Small Town Texas Firemen: Contemporary Hero or Mythical Figure," Michael E. McClellan, Abilene

"Publishing Without Perishing: How to Aid and Abet Your Editor," Trudy McMurrin, Dallas

"Elephant Ears in the Churchyard," Al Lowman, Stringtown

"Mechanical Macho: The Current Craze for Customizing Pickups," Kenneth W. Davis, Lubbock

Sixth session:
Presiding: Pat Jasper, Austin
"Son of Night Horse Nightmare," Paul Patterson, Crane
"Hog Drovers: The Why and How of Hog Drives," Lora B. Garrison, Utopia
"Miguel Acosta: Instrument Maker," James C. McNutt, San Antonio
Business meeting, Joe Graham presiding

Sonovagun Stew. PTFS XLVI. Francis E. Abernethy, editor. Dallas: SMU Press, 1985.

CONTENTS

Seventieth Annual Meeting, held at Jefferson on March 27 through 29, 1986 hosted by East Texas State University, Richland College and Paris Junior College.

Officers
President: Melvin Mason, Huntsville
Vice-President: Jim Harris, Hobbs, New Mexico
Secretary-Editor: Francis E. Abernethy, Nacogdoches
Treasurer: Edwin W. Gaston, Nacogdoches
Directors: Sylvia Grider, College Station; Charles Linck, Commerce; Elmer Kelton, San Angelo; Joe Graham, Millican; Lou Rodenberger, Baird
Councilors: Ernest Speck, Alpine; Art Hendrix, Commerce; Jim McNutt, San

Antonio; Faye Leeper, Midland; Loraine Anderson, Ruston, Louisiana; Connie Ricci, Abilene

Program

Thursday, March 27

Plantation Party, Freeman Plantation, hosted by the Historical Jefferson Foundation

Hootenanny

Friday, March 28

Session I

Chairs: Sylvia Grider, College Station, and Lou Rodenberger, Baird

"Through the Mists," Martha Emmons, Waco

"The Family Saga," Lawrence Clayton, Abilene

"The Widow's Revenge—The Genesis and Development of a Tale in Bell County," Kenneth Davis, Lubbock

Session II

Chairs: Mary Harris, Hobbs, Ernestine Sewell, Commerce

"The Galloping Gourmet," John O. West, El Paso

"Mexican-American Lime Kilns: The Limits of Folk Technology," Joe Graham, Millican

"A High Toned Woman," Joyce Roach, Keller

Session III

Chair: Jim Harris, Hobbs

"Rural Customs in 'The Specialist,'" F.E. Abernethy, Nacogdoches

"The Unicorn in Texas," James W. Byrd, Commerce

"Eats," James Ward Lee, Denton

Session IV

Chair, Mary Nye, Dallas

"A Key of Golden: Brief Encounters Remembered," Mrs. John Q. Anderson, Ruston, Louisiana

"The Message Makers," Faye Leeper, Midland

"The Twilight of a Legend," Olivia M. Nichols, Dallas

Banquet: Toastmaster, Melvin Mason; Speaker. Wyatt Moore

Saturday, March 29

Session V

Chairs: Annette Milton, Dallas, and Margie Hendrix, Commerce

"Texas Baptistry Paintings: Landscape, Doctrine, Mysticism," Jack Welch, Abilene

"Showdown at Sunup," Paul Patterson, Crane

"Praise the Lord and Toss the Cow Chips," Ernest Speck, Alpine

Session VI

Chair: Sarah Greene, Gilmer

"Folk Dramatic Elements and Ends From the Boy Scout Campfire," J. Rhett Rushing, Houston

"Elephant Ears in Aspic," Al Lowman, San Antonio

"A Rose Blooms in the Desert: The Santa Rita No. 1," Edward Roland, Midland

"Learning to Dance," Palmer H. Olsen, Clifton

Business session

Seventy-first annual meeting, Galveston, Texas, April 16–18, 1987. Key Largo Resort Hotel
Officers
President: Jim Harris, Hobbs, New Mexico
Vice President: Lou Rodenberger, Baird
Secretary-Editor: F.E. Abernethy, Nacogdoches
Treasurer: Edwin W. Gaston, Nacogdoches
Directors: Melvin R. Mason, Charles E. Linck, Elmer Kelton, Joe Graham
Councilors: Jim McNutt, Faye Leeper, Loraine Anderson, Connie Ricci, Olivia Nichols, William N. Stokes
Program
Thursday, April 16
Hootenanny
Friday, April 17
Session I
Chair: Margaret Waring, Comanche
"Western Folk Images in Contemporary Advertising," Lawrence Clayton, Abilene
"The Lone Ranger Rides Again," Connie Ricci, Abilene
"Are You a Real Cowboy? That All Depends: Living Country in the City," Gretchen Lutz, Pasadena
"Visual Mythology in America," B.W. Aston, Abilene
Session II
Chair: Jim McNutt, San Antonio
"The Folksong Scholarship of Dorothy Scarborough," Sylvia Grider, College Station
"The Surrogate Foe," Faye Leeper, Midland
"Sons of the Knights of the Yellow Rose: Latterday Mythmakers or Spoofers?," James G. Smith, Beaumont
"A Rural Mail Carrier," Milton McAfee, Dallas
Session III
Chair: Sarah Greene, Gilmer
"Alberto Ramirez, Bricoleur par excellence," Joe Graham, College Station
"The Spanish Romaneria," Charles B. Martin, Denton
"Spooks at the pass of the North," John O. West, El Paso
"Some of the Folk," Ernest Speck, Alpine
Session IV
Chair: James Leeper, Midland
"Bodies and Souls: Some Partings of the Twain," Kenneth Davis, Lubbock
"A Quiet Life in 'The South Side of Heaven,'" Mrs. John Q. Anderson, Ruston, LA
"Farm Horse to Farmall: Folklore and Recollection," Dean Nichols, Dallas
"The Perils of Pauline—Rural Style," Pauline Crittenden, Dallas
Banquet: Speaker: Rudolfo Anaya, Albuquerque, New Mexico
Saturday, April 18
Session V
Chair: Olivia Nichols, Dallas
"Identifying Folk Art: The Huntsville Project," Melvin Mason, Huntsville

"Tender Loving Care: A Video Documentary about Folk Artist Manny Gammage and the Texas Hatters," Martha Hartzog and Paul Congo, Austin
"Childhood Frolics and Floggings in Early 20th Century," Palmer Olsen, Clifton
Session VI
Chair: Betty Casey, Kerrville
"Hallelujah, I'm a Bum," Paul Patterson, Crane
"Texas Folklorists in Australia," F.E. Abernethy, Nacogdoches
"Fugitive Elephant Ears in the Cotton Patch," Al Lowman, San Antonio
Bill Brett, Storyteller
Business session

Hoein' the Short Rows. PTFS XLVII. Francis Edward Abernethy, editor. Dallas, SMU Press, 1987.

CONTENTS

Seventy-second annual meeting, held at Lubbock, Texas, March 31–April 2, 1988.
Officers
President: Lou Rodenberger, Baird
Vice President: Sarah Greene, Gilmer
Secretary-Editor: F.E. Abernethy, Nacogdoches

Treasurer: Edwin W. Gaston, Nacogdoches
General Counsel: William N. Stokes, Dallas
Directors: Joe S. Graham, Kingsville; Melvin R. Mason, Huntsville; James C. McNutt, San Antonio; Faye Leeper, Midland; Jim Harris, Hobbs, New Mexico
Councilors: Connie Ricci, Abilene; Olivia Nichols, Dallas; William N. Stokes, Dallas; Kenneth W. Davis, Lubbock; Tony C. Clark, Paris; Al Lowman, Huntsville
Program
Thursday March 31
Hootenanny
Friday April 1
Session I
Chair: Robert J. Duncan
"A Roof of One's Own," Frances, Rosemary, and Walter Killam, Denton
"Decorative Farm and Ranch Entrances," Mary Harris, Hobbs, New Mexico
"Tall Tales from Down Under: Storm Cellar Wisdom," Faye Leeper, Midland
"Eden's Greens," Joyce Roach, Keller
Session II
Chair: Ernestine Sewell
"Innocence Personified," Palmer Olsen, Clifton
"Silver Bullets: Witchcraft and Demonology in Central Texas in the early 20th Century," Kenneth Davis, Lubbock
"From Afoot to Whetrock: Folk-say on Dreary Hollow," Ernest Speck, Alpine
Texas Fiddle Favorites for Banjo and Mandolin: A Demonstration, Alan Munde and Joe Carr, Levelland
Session III
Chair: Paul Patterson
"Hero, Villian or Temporary Prince," Jeri Tanner, Lubbock
"And Lo! To Vernon, Texas there came: the Con Man, the Bootlegger Man and the Music Man," William N. Stokes, Dallas
"Raking up the Elephant Ears," Al Lowman, San Marcos
"Lifestyles of the Poor and Infamous; or How Fentress Overcame the Handicap of Living Downstream from Staples," William P. Barber, San Marcos
Session IV
"A Tribute to Martha Emmons," Francis E. Abernethy, Nacogdoches; James W. Byrd, Commerce; James Ward Lee, Denton
Tour, Southwest Collection and Peter Hurd Mural, Texas Tech University Campus
Banquet, Elmer Kelton, speaker
Saturday, April 2
Session V
Chair: Loraine Anderson
"A Popurrí of Mexican American Folklore," John O. West, El Paso
"The World Writ Small: Mexican Folk Toys," Joe Graham, Kingsville
"The German Volkfest in Texas," W.M. Von Maszewski, Pasadena
"Tell It Like It Is: The Adventure of Ezekiel Gibbs, Texas Black Folk Artist," Cecile Greer Burns, Lubbock

Session VI
Chair: Mary Nye
"The Faultless Starch Library," Ellisene Davis, Keller
"From Surviving to Having Fun: The Changing Role of Some Folk Skills and Crafts," Lawrence Clayton, Abilene
"Glen Rose 'Shine," Janet Jeffery, Austin
"Chores of Pioneer Children; or, Idle Hands are the Devil's Workshop," Lora B. Garrison, Utopia
Business session

The Seventy-third annual meeting, March 23–25, 1989, Uvalde, sponsored by Southwest Texas Junior College.
Officers
President: Sarah Greene, Gilmer
Vice President: Al Lowman, San Marcos
Secretary-Editor: F.E. Abernethy, Nacogdoches
Treasurer: Edwin W. Gaston, Nacogdoches
General Counsel: William N. Stokes, Dallas
Directors: Melvin R. Mason, Huntsville; James C. McNutt, San Antonio; Faye Leeper, Midland; Jim Harris, Hobbs, New Mexico; Lou Rodenberger, Baird
Councilors: William N. Stokes, Dallas; Tony C. Clark, Paris; Kenneth W. Davis, Lubbock; Lora B. Garrison, Utopia, Mary Harris, Hobbs, New Mexico
Program
Thursday, March 23
Tours, Chaparrosa Ranch, Garner Museum, Grand Opera House
Reception
Schawe Indian Dancers
Hootenanny
Friday, March 24
Welcome: Uvalde County Judge Bill Mitchell
Session I, Texas Musical Traditions
Chair, James McNutt
"Houston Creoles and Zodico," John Minton, San Antonio
"Texas Fiddlers: A Documentary," Michael Schoenecke and Ashton Thornhill, Lubbock
"Conjunto and the Mexican-American Community," Ward S. Albro, Kingsville
"Native Music of Texas," John Wheat
Session II, Public Folk Arts Programming
Chair: Margaret Waring
"Texas-Mexican Folk Catholicism: Personal Devotion and its Public Presentation," Kay Turner, Austin
"Apprenticeships in the Folk Arts: Lessons on Folk Learning," Pat Jasper, Austin
"A Legacy of Forms: Folk Art in the Schools," Betsy Peterson, Austin
"Other Voices, Other Rooms: Some Comments About Public Folklore Program From a University Perspective," Carl Lindahl, University of Houston

Session III, The Sense of Place
Chair: Glen Lich
"Our Town: A Dialogue of Memories," Joyce Roach, Keller, and Robert L. Flynn, San Antonio
"Toward an Understanding of Place for the Southwestern Indian," M. Jane Young, Albuquerque
"Over Where I Growed Up," Bill Brett, Hull-Daisetta
Session IV, Border Folk Medicine
Chair, John West
"The Breadth of Mexican-American Folk Medicine," John O. West, El Paso
"Curanderismo in the Eagle Pass Region," Sandra Cruz, Eagle Pass
"Knowledge About Folk Medicine Among Students in Alice High School," Elizabeth Galindo, Alice
"Medicinal Herbs in the Lower Rio Grande Valley and Tamaulipas, Mexico," Tony Zavaleta, Brownsville
"Medicinal Herbs: Placebos or Biomedicine?" Joe S. Graham, Bishop
Banquet
Welcome: Dr. Jimmy Goodson, President of SWTJC
Film: "The Newton Brothers of Uvalde"
Saturday, March 25
Session V, Texas Personalities
Chair: Johnnye Sturcken
"Cactus Jack Garner as Folk Hero," Lora B. Garrison, Utopia
"Brush Country, Backeros, and Hamlet's Ghost," Paul C. Stone, New Haven,Connecticut
"Ben Carlton Mead: Portrait of an Artist," Jack Duncan, McKinney
Business Sesson
Session VI, Potpourri
Chair: Lee Haile
"Folklore and History as a Subject of the Writer's Craft," Max Martinez, San Antonio
"Sniding and Being Snided: Horse Trader Tales," Dick Heaberlin, San Marcos
"Watch the Fords Go By: The Automobile Hits Old Bell County," Ken Davis, Lubbock
"You Can Tell a Scout From Texas," Rebecca Carnes, Slaton

Texas Toys and Games. PTFS XLVIII. Francis Edward Abernethy, editor. Dallas: Southern Methodist University Press, 1989.

CONTENTS

Reese Kennedy, artist for *Built in Texas*

Loraine Anderson, Mary Elizabeth Nye, and Bill Stokes

Jim Harris and Hawk

Don Swadley

Jean Granberry Schnitz

Gene and Marynell Young

John Lightfoot

James Ward Lee

Palmer Olsen

Acayla, Sierra, and Lee Haile

Rosemary Killam, Lee Haile, Jcyce Roach, Ab Abernethy, unidentified, and Don Swadley

Robert Flynn

Ross McSwain

Lee Haile, Jim and Mary Harris, and Lou Rodenberger

Kent Biffle of the *Dallas Morning News*

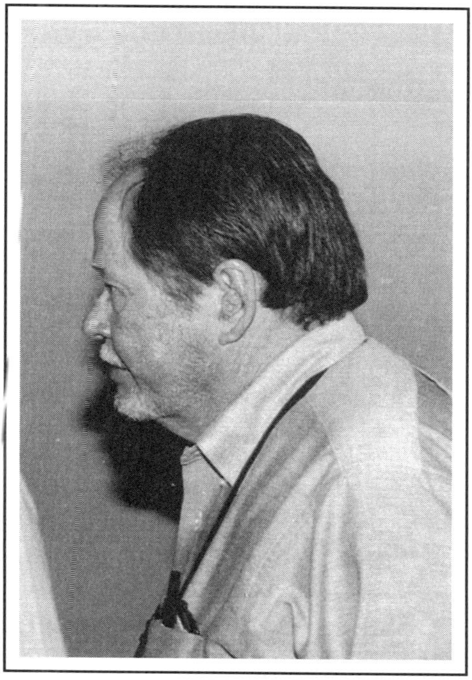

L. Patrick Hughes

Claudia Ball, Director of the Texas Folklife Festival and hostess for the San Antonio meeting in 1980

Don Swadley, Jim Lee, Jim Harris, Ab Abernethy

Fran Vick, Joyce Roach, Ann Gibson

Archie McDonald

Olivia Nichols

Dean Nichols

Delight Roach

Betty Casey

Jerry Hunt and Patrick Dearen

III
University of North Texas Press: 1990 to 2000

3 IN 4 YEARS
CHAMPION
22
impeachment
NELSON MANDELA

1990

Al Lowman
President 1989–90 at Kingsville
Manager of Lowman Ranch at San Marcos, Lt. Col. Field Artillery (retired), former Senior Research Associate at the Institute of Texan Cultures, Fellow of the Texas State Historical Association, bibliophile, author of *At the Pass with Carl Hertzog* and *Printing Arts in Texas*, 1975

This last decade of the Second Millennium started off with some real surprises. The Berlin Wall fell and Germany was reunited for the first time since the end of World War II. Soviet troops withdrew from Czechoslovakia, which was the beginning of a retreat and collapse of Communism throughout eastern Europe. I am sparked to remember Kruschev's communist threat to democracy, "We will bury you!" In 1990 Nelson Mandela was freed from prison after three decades, signaling the beginning of the end of apartheid in South Africa. And conversely, President George Bush was forced to send troops to stand by in Arabia after Saddam Hussein and Iraq occupied Kuwait. 1990 was a significant year.

The Texas Folklore Society entered the last decade of the twentieth century with a new secretary-assistant editor, Carolyn Satterwhite, a new publisher, Fran Vick of the University of North Texas Press in Denton, and total cash assets of $112,655.25. These facts and figures did not solve all of the Society's problems, but they certainly improved its prospects.

The Society met at Kingsville on April 12–14, 1990. The meeting was presided over by Al Lowman of Stringtown and San Marcos and hosted by Joe Graham and Texas A&I. Al is a bibliophile who spent much of his professional career as a researcher with the Institute of Texan Cultures at San Antonio. He is also the Sage of San Marcos and Staples, Texas, and the purveyor of Staples' wit and wisdom.

Members began the meeting with a pilgrimage to the grave and shrine of Don Pedrito Jaramillo, the Healer of Los Olmos, made famous by Wilson Hudson's PTFS 24–1951, *The Healer of Los Olmos and Other Mexican Lore*. Our other excursion was a visit to the headquarters of the King Ranch. Another special event occurred Thursday night with the premier of Melvin Mason's film "Come Hungry, Come Thirsty," a documentary of religious camp meetings. For the ultimate seasoning, Joe Graham hired a band and threw a baile for members after the Friday night banquet.

Because of its south Texas setting the meeting was heavy on Tex-Mex presentations. We also had a session dedicated to Paul Patterson, longtime member and cowboy writer from Crane and points west.

My last serious visit to the Valley had been in 1963 when I attended a Texas Herpetological Society meeting near Kingsville. We caught, identified, and released hundreds (it seemed like) of snakes, many of which we caught driving the back roads at night. In 1990 on my way home I drove the back roads for fifty miles and did not see a single snake. The species had become endangered in a generation.

The Society's move to the University of North Texas Press was easy and comfortable because the Society had worked with Fran Vick and E-Heart Press for four publications from 1979 to 1983. The move to UNT Press was profitable as well as fitting because of the generosity of Keith Gregory, Director of SMU Press. Keith transferred gratis the entire PTFS inventory from SMU to UNT Press. In a letter to Fran dated May 23, 1990, Keith writes: "On 1 June 1990 the thirty-four annual publications of the Texas Folklore Society (TFS) that are still available from Southern Methodist University Press (list of publications attached) and the related ANALYTICAL INDEX will be transferred to the University of North Texas Press." This good financial fortune was another sign of and reason for our improving prospects.

Concerning that felicitous transfer Fran Vick recently (January 28, 2000) wrote:

"When the University of North Texas Press was formed in 1987, with the first books being published in 1989, Keith Gregory called me and asked if I wanted to take the publication of the TFS books back. Suzanne had already left and was battling that ferocious cancer that finally killed her. As Keith said, Suzanne was the one who was interested in Texas folklore and without her at the press there was no one to take the books through publication. I, of course, jumped at the offer and called the Society about it. Then came the most wonderful and generous gesture of all. Keith transferred ALL of the Texas Folklore Society publications to the University of North Texas Press! That included all of the facsimile books from 1916 to the books SMU Press had produced under Allen Maxwell, et al, to the brand new books that Trudy and Suzanne had produced. So this new UNT Press now had a built-in backlist of books to build a publication list on, with the promise of a TFS publication each year thereafter. It was a tremendous gift to us and one that our Vice President of Fiscal Affairs is still trying to figure out. He was sure that we would get some whopping bill for all the books that would put UNT Press in the red forever. That generous gift is what started me on my quest of getting all of the TFS publications under one umbrella. We finally accomplished that when Encino Press transferred the books they had to UNT Press, but it certainly took a long time. I had already transferred all rights from my own E-Heart Press to UNT Press with the reprinting of *Legendary Ladies* and *Singin' Texas*. *Built in Texas* will be reprinted this coming season (2000). I have *T for Texas* on the Lightning Books list for reprints on demand."

The book for 1990 was a miscellany entitled *The Bounty of Texas* (PTFS 49), published at a cost of $10,483.53. The Society was due a miscellany. Every two or three years we publish a miscellany to include the best papers that were presented at meetings and some papers that were submitted directly to the editor. Our policy has been from the beginning to consider papers from members first. This policy is based upon the fact that Society membership fees pay for the Society's publications. We sometimes solicit papers from specialists who are not members, but that is rare.

The lead paper for *The Bounty of Texas* was submitted by a member but written by a non-member. Roland Broaddus of Dallas called me in the summer of 1983 and told me that he had a handwritten manuscript from his cousin that described his cousin's experiences as a trapper in Texas during the 1920s. I was interested, and later that year he sent the typed manuscript. It was a great story, readably written, detailing R. A. "Rusty" Hill's years of living off the bounty of the woods, and it became the lead story and title story for this volume.

During layout of *Bounty* we had planned to have a running head of the title of each article. Through some oversight by all four! of the proofreaders, "Bounty of the Woods," Rusty Hill's running head, became the running head of every article in the book. A friend pointed out this error the day he received the book. I thanked him for his close reading, hung up, and screamed. Every editor or author wishes he could have one more chance of revision after the book is published.

Jim Lee told Martha Emmons that she would live so long that somebody would have to shoot her on Judgment Day. Jim missed it a couple of years, and Martha died on February 22, 1990. She had been a participating TFS member since 1924. Jim wrote a eulogy for Martha Emmons in *Texas Books in Review* (Vol. X, No. 1, p. 16, Spring 1990) which he titled "Martha Emmons Will Go To Heaven—If She Wants To." Martha was an institution at Baylor and in the Texas Folklore Society. Both were less without her. Martha's dear friend, Ann Miller of Waco, wrote this loving elegy.

HERSELF
"Come dance with me in Ireland." —Yeats

You kept death at a distance
for years he had wanted the next
dance and this time when he
offered his hand you took it,

breathless. And then time meant
nothing to you who had kept time so
lightly you seemed almost glad it was
the day for taking hands, for two

stepping into another room they
said we couldn't enter. Here in
this room still at your bedside I
keep time by riffling through

the daily news: laws still being
challenged, children born, games won
and lost. Hallmark, the paper says,
wants us to send an Irish card

this March. The crossword puzzle
is empty space, here is the pencil
you would have used to give it
words. Old friend, already I miss

the dance of your words, I need
your voice. Listen, it is so
quiet so quiet
here.

Here
birds announce returning spring, we
turn to one green brightening glance.
Tell me, does the dancer or the dance
make the dry grass sing?

Ann Miller on Martha Emmons Day

1991

Kenneth W. Davis
President 1990–91 at San Marcos
Professor Emeritus of English at Texas Tech University, now Liaison Officer for retired faculty and staff, chronicler of Old Bell County, with Lawrence Clayton edited *Horsing Around: Contemporary Cowboy Humor*

This was the year of the Persian Gulf War, which Saddam Hussein promised the world would be the "Mother" of all battles and the annihilation of the Western Satan. It was not quite that. United Nations forces began their attack on January 16, 1991, and Kuwait was freed and Iraqi forces were surrounded or pushed back away from the Kuwait border by February 27. We are still debating whether or not we should have gone all the way to Baghdad. The enduring hero who came out of the Persian Gulf War was General Colin Powell, a very dignified and reserved man who could probably have been the first black president of the United States, had he (and his wife) so chosen.

This 1991 was also the year that we rediscovered World War II on the fiftieth anniversary of Pearl Harbor. Movies, TV series, books, symposia, and other celebrations had WWII vets talking about their greatest experience for the next four years.

The seventy-fifth annual Texas Folklore Society meeting was held March 28–30, 1991, in San Marcos, presided over by Kenneth Davis of Texas Tech in Lubbock and hosted by Southwest Texas State University under the arrangements of Rollo and Sylvia Newsom. Besides rounding up cowboys for west Texas poetry symposia, President Ken Davis is the official chronicler of outrageous tales from old Bell County. Dick Holland, director of the Southwestern Writers' Collection in the SWTSU library, invited the TFS members to a reception in his new premises on Thursday night, and the members were treated to a picnic on the banks of the San Marcos River at Friday noon. On Thursday afternoon Al Lowman and Bill Barber conducted a tour of Staples and Fentress and pointed out spots where buildings used to stand and where a lot of things happened.

What emerged as the main concern at the business meeting was the consciousness of the Society's membership maturity. Members looked about them and saw a room full of senior citizens, of more grandparents than parents, and few young people. One of the causes of this was that the academic field of folklore was not as well populated as it had been in the Sixties and Seventies. Fewer folklore courses were being taught on the university level, and fewer students were involved. Another cause was the national phenomenon of increasing lifespans and an aging America. The Society's approach to a solution was to encourage student papers at TFS meetings by paying students up to $150 for travel and lodging expenses. Recruiting new, young members has always been a concern of the TFS, and members' hearts leap up when a new presenter with a new topic steps up to the lectern.

The membership book for 1991, *Hecho en Tejas* (Made in Texas) (PTFS 50), was edited by Joe S. Graham, folklorist and anthropologist at Texas A&I University in Kingsville and research associate with the John E. Conner Museum. *Hecho* was a rich and beautiful book, a fitting Golden Anniversary publication. The Society had published fifty of its own volumes in its seventy-five years of existence, a fitting tribute to a productive existence.

Joe Graham was an Aggie, an electrical engineering major living in sin, when he saw the light under the tutelage of TFS members John Q. Anderson and Sid Cox. He turned over his life to folklore at his first TFS meeting in 1964. He received a Master's in English at Brigham Young University with a thesis on folk narratives, after which he taught at the University of Texas at El Paso under John O. West and at Sul Ross, where he worked with Ernest Speck and Elton Miles. He served as Folklorist in Residence at the Institute of Texan Cultures, followed by a year of folklore fieldwork with a grant from the Texas Committee for the Humanities. He taught at Texas A&M and is now at Texas A&I. This man has been well raised academically.

Hecho en Tejas was the result of Joe Graham's years of interest and research in Mexican culture and in material culture. Joe grew up around Tejanos on ranches in the Big Bend. He did his Ph.D. in Mexican-American folklore under Don Américo Paredes and at Kingsville was in the midst of the richest traditions of Mexican material culture in the state. Joe hosted the annual TFS meeting in Kingsville in 1990, and one section of the program was on Mexican-American material culture, papers done mainly by his students. That was the inspiration and beginning of *Hecho en Tejas*.

This editor's contribution to the 1990 Kingsville meeting, *Hecho en Tejas*, and Joe's horsehair rope projects was to drive to an abattoir in Palestine and purchase twenty-five horse tails. I made the purchase, tossed the bundle of hair and hide in the back of my pickup, and headed home. It was summertime and my freight smelled! Bad! I was expecting buzzards to be following me. Every time I stopped, the smell caught up with me and poured into the cab. When I got home I winched out that huge hank of hair under a shed off the barn and sacked it in garbage bags. I used a dozen garbage bags before I finally got the smell confined enough to box those tails and send them on to Joe. I got a horsehair hatband out of that experience, which took several weeks to clear the sinuses of the horse-tail smell.

The editor and Carolyn Fiedler Satterwhite, office secretary, the Society's treasurer, and assistant editor from 1989 to date

1992

Jeri Tanner (1926–1998)
President 1991–92 at McKinney
Associate Professor Emeritus of English at Texas Tech University, formerly X-ray technician and President of Arkansas Society of X-ray Technicians

All of the years run together in a great river flow, with highly special times popping up periodically to mark the passage. Sometimes we have to go back and find these pop-up episodes so that we will have something with which we can relate the year. 1992 was the year that my five-year-old grandson drove everybody crazy singing "Achy Breaky Heart." Or more generally, that was the year we celebrated the five hundredth anniversary of Columbus's discovery of America. The *Niña*, the *Pinta*, and the *Santa Maria* docked in Corpus Christi. Great debates were staged over who really did discover America, and we made much moaning on the effects of European diseases on native Americans, total population losses occurring in some cases. All that aside, Columbus's discovery was the beginning of our phase of American western civilization, and it is proper that we recognized and remembered what happened. We remember that year.

Jeri Tanner (1926–1998) of Texas Tech University, Lubbock, presided at the 1992 meeting. Jeri had worked diligently as local arranger for our meeting in Lubbock, as program chairman for the 1991 meeting in San Marcos, and as president of this year's meeting in McKinney. This was President Jeri's opportunity to greet and speak and be charming, and she caught a cold and could barely whisper, even at the banquet where she presided over the massed membership.

We met that year on April 16–18 at the Holiday Inn in McKinney. The meeting was hosted by Collin County Community College, the Center for Texas Studies (Jim Lee, Director) at the University of North Texas, and by the University of North Texas Press (Fran Vick, Director). Fran created the printed program, which had a Charles Shaw sketch of TFS founders John Lomax and Leonidas Payne, with the founding spirit George Lyman Kittredge hovering in the background. Jim Lee gave a beautifully thoughtful banquet speech, entitled "The Uses of Folklore."

Hecho en Tejas, the PTFS 50 for 1991, finally got to members in March! of 1992.

The book for 1992 was actually the long promised history of the TFS, quite simply named (on the advice of Ione Brooks) *The Texas Folklore Society, 1909–1943, Volume I of III*, (PTFS 51–1992). I had been contemplating writing the Society history ever since I became secretary-editor in 1971. I knew that it must be done eventually.

As is frequently the case, the history's actual beginning was the result of a chance of circumstance. At the end of the 1984 Huntsville business meeting, Jack Duncan and John O. West asked that all the Society's programs be published in some upcoming miscellany. This was a simple enough request. They wanted to know what folklore topics members had been interested in and had been talking about since that first TFS gathering in 1911. When I returned to the Society's office I immediately set Marlene Adams, then the TFS secretary, to typing up all past TFS meeting programs for inclusion in the next PTFS.

That stack of programs made an impressive list and one that activated the typing of another list, the tables of contents of PTFSs that followed the programs. I was prompted to making this second list because I wanted to know the relation of the publications' contents to the meetings' contents.

That great flurry of list typing led me to wanting to know more about the people who made up these programs and tables of contents. And that was the beginning of numerous trips to the Barker Center at The University of Texas and days of sifting through the TFS files which are stored there.

Next step: I now had all of this data—the previously mentioned lists, the minutes of meetings, financial records, correspondence—which kept flashing pictures at me of people and meetings and tours and singings and dancings. Before long I had enough material to make a pretty good entry for each year. And really, this was all I had set out to do, to get in one place the records and happenings of the Society from 1909 to date.

I was next led astray by Leonidas Payne's pamphlet, "I Was Here When the Woods Were Burnt." Payne describes the seminal meeting between him and John Lomax so vividly that I was caught up in an atmosphere of social history that I felt compelled to continue. Therefore, I tried to entwine the goings on of the Texas Folklore Society with Gibson Girls and World War I and the Roaring Twenties and the Crash and Depression and World War II—and with the songs they sang and the movies they went to—and the clothes they wore and the cars they drove—and life. These were the settings in which all these meetings that Duncan and West were interested in took place.

The result, of course, was that considerably more space was required per year's entry than I had thought probable. In addition to which, I found myself sometimes waxing philosophical about the goings on within and without the Society and occupied a few more precious signatures.

All of this flurry of TFS activities became very alive to me. I saw the members listening and having singalongs and sightseeings. I labored with Dobie and Mody and Ransom as they struggled to put together an annual. I read letters of anger and sadness and excitement and responded sympathetically to names that came alive and let me listen to them and feel some of what they felt.

I worked diligently collecting pictures and early illustrations, because I wanted to see what these early folklorists looked like and I believed that their likenesses should be printed for future folklorists.

The text and the illustrations for TFS I were with the publisher and designer in the spring of 1992. In May I received the layout about five days before I left for Indonesia. It was a mess and you could have heard me yelling in Bali! In those few days I had left I laid the book out generally and asked Fran to get us a designer. She did. She got a young lady named Caissa Dowes in Austin, with whom I could communicate. We finally got a layout that everybody liked. The layout for this first volume of the TFS was important because we were setting a pattern for the ensuing volumes. The artwork for this first volume was also important, and Charles Shaw of Dripping Springs began his stint with the TFS by drawing a beautiful dust jacket and historically evocative illustrations for each chapter heading. As usual, the 1992 book got to members in January 1993. The cost of producing 2046 volumes was $11,090.67, but that number was not too frightening in view of the Society's balance of $133,948.35 at the beginning of that year.

Fran Vick, Director of the University of North Texas Press

1993

Dick Heaberlin
President 1992–93 at San Angelo
Professor of English at
Southwest Texas State University

If you cannot remember 1993 specifically, I will remind you that that was the April when we came home for lunch and saw the Branch Davidian compound beginning to burn at the north end. And as we watched, the flames swept south through the huge frame structure until it was a whirlwind of fire. The Mt. Carmel structure burned to a fine ash and incinerated seventy-three men, women, and children. The catastrophe was the end of a fifty-one-day shootout and standoff between the forces of the establishment and a religious splinter group of religious disestablishmentarians. Most Americans are still ambivalent about the cause and effect of that conflict.

Bill Clinton was inaugurated as president for his second term, and the Cowboys defeated Buffalo in the Super Bowl.

The 1993 correspondence files begin with early reader responses to TFS I, most of which were positive. And I liked the book myself, which is not always the case with TFS publications. But nestled in among the roses were mentions of factual errors in the book, some of which still make me sweat. Readers found misspelled names, wrong dates, misplaced modifiers, ad inf. I promised readers that I would begin TFS II with an errata sheet. And I did.

The Society met in San Angelo for its seventy-seventh meeting. We met at the Holiday Inn on April 8–10 with Dick Heaberlin of Southwest Texas State University presiding and Mildred Boren as local arranger. We had the usual good papers with one or two real dogs in the litter. One of the main things that I remember about that meeting was Mary Elizabeth Nye and her friend Bruce Hunter getting completely exercised about the smoking that was going on in the motel halls between sessions. We had emotional speeches, a brief debate, and a motion. The result was that Society members who smoked resolved that they would be sensitive to the non-smokers. The whole proceeding was a good exercise in Robert's Rules of Order.

We also had a couple of presentations with slides, during which the presenters looked at the slide picture and talked instead of talking directly to the audience. This prompted member Leroy Brown, who was a bit hard of hearing, into a frenzied order to speakers to "Talk into the mike! If you are a speaker, SPEAK!" This was a small part of a message I received after the meeting, but you get the gist. Leroy's remarks were included in the minutes of the meeting.

And to mark the advent of a new generation, Delight Roach, daughter of longtime member Joyce Roach, gave her first paper, a delightful discussion of the legendary Billie Sol Estes.

The book for 1993 was a traditional miscellany entitled *Corners of Texas*. It was a large book, 295 pages, and it was designed by Nancy Land of Publications Development Company of Crockett, Texas. We printed 2023 copies for $16,082.95. I liked the book design very much, and the *Fort Worth Star-Telegram* Sunday business section published a large front-page picture of a recently retired business man, lying on his bed with *Corners of Texas* propped on his belt buckle. We had some good publicity for *Corners*, mainly because it was a good book, very rich in content, and we had good sales. Unfortunately Nancy Land and I had an unsolvable disagreement over a five-hundred-dollar charge, and our literary relationship ended with this publication.

The title for *Corners* came from two places. First, the title came from a Frank Dobie pamphlet. Dobie had wanted to create a Corner of Texas at the University of Texas. He wanted a collection of Texana in a specially created and decorated library room that would reflect Texas culture and its heritage. Dobie made his plea for this special Texas corner in a 1938 pamphlet entitled "A Corner Forever Texas."

Secondly, Dick Holland, founder and director of The Southwest Writers Collection at Southwest Texas State University titled his lead article "A Corner Forever Texas: The Southwest Writers Collection." Dick talks about the Collection and Bill Wittliff's part in the founding, mainly Bill's purchase at the Dobie auction of boxes of Dobie manuscripts and memorabilia. These Dobie manuscripts are the center of the Southwest Collection, and Dobie's Forever Corner came into being with the Southwest Collection.

Corners begins with Holland's article, which is followed by three more articles that deal with some aspect of the history of the Texas Folklore Society: Nolan Porterfield on John Lomax, Paul Stone on Dobie and the American Folklore Society, and Al Lowman on Carl Hertzog and the TFS. The editor was in the midst of TFS history at the time, and these lead articles were dear to his heart—and a valuable addition to Society history.

TFS founder John A. Lomax received a lot of attention during 1993. Nolan Porterfield was in the midst of his biographical research and was interviewing sources for his *Last Cavalier: The Life and Times of John A. Lomax*. The Bosque County Historical Commission had a John A. Lomax gathering on the banks of the Bosque River, near Meridian, where they honored the Lomax family and sang the cowboy songs that John Lomax had spent his early life collecting.

Elton Miles, the sage of the Big Bend, was not able to make the Easter meetings during his last years, but as a continually practicing folklorist he responded to the papers, two of which were published in *Corners of Texas*. Adding to George Ewing's talk on the eternal uses of a forked stick, Elton told about his grandfather's using a forked stick to twist a rabbit that had run into its hollow: "On his knees Grandad stuck the fork into the hideaway, probed and twisted for less than a minute, then pulled out the stick, rabbit and all. He had 'wound up' the rabbit's loose hide on the fork" (August 28, 1993). Earlier, Elton had responded to Rana Williamson's drouth stories with his story about spotty west Texas showers: "A cowboy leaned his double-barreled shotgun against a rock, and it came a shower. When it was over one barrel was brim-full of water and the other was still dry and ready to fire."

Ranchers would say to their friends on parting, "I've gotta go dust out my rain gauge" (August 26, 1993).

A real folklorist cannot sit still and be out-folked, even if he (or she!) has to lie.

Bill Wittliff and Dick Holland in a Corner of Texas, the Southwestern Writers Collection at Southwest Texas State University in San Marcos. Bill Wittliff was responsible for the founding of the Southwest Writers Collection and Dick Holland was its first director.

1994

Mildred Boren Sentell
President 1993–94 at Victoria
Taught English at Angelo State, President of the West Texas Historical Association, professional mother and skilled housewife

This was the year that the Cowboys defeated the Buffalo Bills again in the Super Bowl. More memorably, 1994 was the year that South Africa ended apartheid and elected the black Nelson Mandela as its president. A devastating earthquake occurred in Los Angeles and surroundings, but California did not crumble and fall off into the Pacific Ocean, as my grandmother predicted.

Henry Wolff was the local arranger when the Society held its seventy-eighth meeting at the Holiday Inn in Victoria from March 31 to April 2, 1994, with Mildred Boren Sentell of Snyder and Angelo State College presiding. Besides the regular proceedings of the meeting, members toured local museums and on Saturday a large contingent met at La Bahia, Col. James Fannin's Fort Defiance at Goliad. Goliad is an impressive historical reconstruction done under the architectural skills of San Augustine's Raiford Stripling.

My focus that year was on the second volume of the history of the Texas Folklore Society, this time from 1943 to 1971. The span of time included the tenures of Mody Boatright and Wilson M. Hudson and included the time and the people of my professors' and parents' generation of TFS folklorists. Most of us came into the Society around 1960, at the height of the academic folklore enthusiasm, and Mody and Wilson and their peers were our academic guides. Most folklorists then were English teachers who had gravitated or had been nudged by department heads into folklore so that the departments could include folklore in its catalog. It was a popular course and classes filled quickly and fully. I had loads of material for the TFS II volume—pictures, papers, dust jackets, reminiscences—and the book was a pleasure to do. We got it out in 1994 to fair reviews, but this TFS history volume did not receive the plaudits that the first volume got.

The University of North Texas Press resurrected two of the Society's out-of-print best sellers in 1993–1994. They were *Singin' Texas* (ExB–18, 1983) and *Legendary Ladies of Texas* (PTFS 43–1981). Fran ran 2,064 *Singin' Texas* for $5,000 and 1,564 copies of *Legendary Ladies* for $7,000.

Another attempt at a volume on the family saga died that year.

Jim Harris ran a survey among members in 1994 on subjects of TFS presentations and publication. Most of the questions dealt with whether the surveyee believed that the TFS was oriented more toward the rural than the urban. Respondents recognized that we dealt with much rural folklore, but that considering the aging generation of members involved, most of them came from a rural pre-WWII environment. These rural experiences were what the members drew from in their research and writing. Most present-day programs, however, are a balanced mixture of the rural and urban, as well as past and present. At the Victoria meeting that year, ten of the sixteen papers given were on modern and/or urban folklore. And we had one whole session on modern urban folklore.

And that was the year, 1994, that I was asked to attend sessions at SFA on sensitivity training. A "mature" TFS member applied to the SFA English department and wrote me, asking about his prospects. I told him that a whole generation of old profs were retiring around this time and that probably the department was looking for new Ph.D.s at the minimum-pay, assistant professor level. I was speaking to him as to a friend. He did not get the job, and he threatened to sue the department because he said (on the basis of what I had said) that he believed that they had discriminated against him on the basis of his age. I would gladly have throttled him, even if it had meant losing a Society member. I lasted about ten minutes in that sensitivity training session, which was an exercise in cliches telling the audience to be kind to one another. But I am sure that now I am a kinder gentler man—except where "he" is concerned.

Jerry Lincecum in the role of his ancestor, Gideon Lincecum

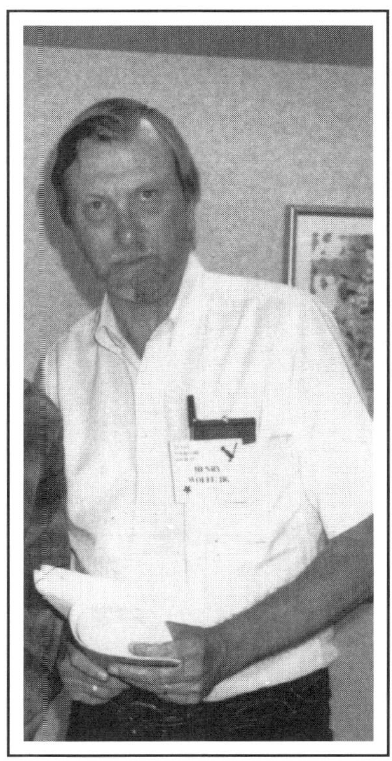

Henry Wolff, Jr., the Society's host in Victoria

1995

Faye Leeper
President 1994–95 at Fort Worth
Taught high school English in Midland and taught at Midland Community College, acted as a European tour guide, began her life with the TFS reading her prize winning student paper at the A&M meeting in 1956

Catastrophes loom as the indices to time, and this year's horror was the Oklahoma City car-bombing. The Alfred P. Murrah Federal Building and several surrounding buildings were demolished and 169 people were killed.

We met in Fort Worth, April 13–14, 1995, in the Green Oaks Inn, a shady island between speedways. Joyce Roach was the hostess for this meeting, and the Society was singularly blessed by the company of a roadrunner—our totem, you know—who wandered about the grounds, visiting with members. He skipped the paper sessions, however.

Faye Leeper of Midland and Irving was TFS president that year. Faye had been a member since 1956, when as Ralph Huston's student her paper won a place in the TFS student paper contest. She gave her first paper that year at A&M. Faye taught English on both high school and college levels, and in 1995 was retired, doing free-lance writing, and conducting European tours.

A significant part of the program was a panel comprised of five teachers of folklore speaking on the topic, "How I define folklore for my students." The panel was a response to many questions by members about the definition of folklore and was also a response to members' papers, many of which drifted off of folklore into history, sociology, and genealogy. A lively discussion among members ensued, and the definition papers became the nucleus for the next folklore miscellany, *Between the Cracks of History: Essays on Teaching and Illustrating Folklore* (PTFS 55–1997).

My own classroom basic definition of folklore for thirty years or more was "Folklore is the traditional knowledge of a culture." Then I spent the rest of the semester trying to explain and illustrate *traditional* and *culture*.

Looking over this year's newsletters, I notice another editorial phenomenon that is familiar because it is recurring. It goes like this: I announce in a newsletter that an upcoming TFS publication will be something in particular; in 1995 I announced in the January newsletter that the book for the year would be an illustrated history of Sacred Harp music. Then the strangest sorts of miscommunications occurred, and I found myself out of communication with the author of the publication. I have as yet to figure out what happened there. Anyhow, we had no Sacred Harp publication, but no member accosted me about this failure. I am still not sure whether this non-response is the result of members not reading their newsletter closely or whether the kindness of members precludes their reminding me of the error. Looking back I remember promises about upcoming books on family sagas, black folklore, and TFS histories that I never made good on.

When the Sacred Harp book fell through the cracks, we turned to other extra-book sources and luckily found the recently published edition of John Erickson's *Through Time and the Valley* (ExB 21–1995), the history and folklore of the Canadian River as it runs through part of the Panhandle of Texas. I grew up on a ranch on the Washita, which is one river south of the Canadian, so that influenced my choice. Another influence was that Erickson was our banquet speaker in Abilene in 1985 and read "Hank the Cowdog" to the great delight of the membership. *Through Time and the Valley* was a happy choice, although I was never happy when I had to use an Extra Book out of necessity.

Two long-time points of conflict arose for discussion in the business meeting. One was the Easter meeting date that became traditional back in 1958, when the Society chose that date to meet so that teachers would have Easter vacation holidays to make it to Alpine and back. Before then, the Society met on the weekend before or after San Jacinto Day, April 21. The vast majority of members wanted to stay with the Easter weekend as our regular time of meeting. The same majority voted against split meeting sessions, with two sessions taking place at the same time. The Society decided, and rightfully so, that all of the papers presented should be available to all of the audience at one time.

I do not see the Society as being especially conservative. I see the Society and its membership as lasting long enough to know what they wanted to do and how they wanted to do it.

Ann Gibson, Joyce Roach, and Georgia Caraway

1996

George W. Ewing
President 1995–96 at Abilene
Head of the Department of English at Abilene Christian College (retired), preacher, singer, and story teller, and author of *The Well-Tempered Lyre* on temperance verse, now doing maintenance work and preaching at a retirement home

This was an election year that boiled down to a race between Republican Bob Dole and the Democratic incumbent Bill Clinton, with Ross Perot yapping around on the fringes. The greatly respected congressman Dole had not a snowball's chance against the glibness of Bill Clinton and the fact that Clinton presided over a nation in the grip of prosperity.

This was another year I had to eat the words from one newsletter when something happened before the next. I concluded the January '96 invitation letter with the call to meet for a joyful Easter in Abilene, and because 1995–96 was a cold winter, I concluded with a call for members to come to Abilene "and thaw!" Texas weather got in the way. White stuff that was easily identified as snow began falling early Friday morning of the meeting. The Abileners, local arranger Lawrence Clayton included, reckoned that this April-Easter snow phenomenon was most unusual, was only a flurry, and would soon pass. They were utterly confounded when the snow continued all day and into the evening. Society members arose Saturday morning to find the west Texas world around Abilene covered in eight to ten inches of snow, and holding. In some places nearby eighteen inches of snow accumulated. The highways were closed and Abilene was snowed in. Members and presenters such as Alan Munde and Joe Carr from Levelland who had planned to come to the meeting on Friday returned the way they came, which cut down on parts of the planned program. Highways were opening on Saturday, but many of us stayed holed up, cozy and warm and enjoying the occasion, until the sun came out on Sunday. Staying in Abilene at the Embassy Suites Hotel was certainly no hardship.

The Society met April 4–6, 1996, with George Ewing of Abilene presiding. George is the Society's chaplain. He is a preacher, he was a teacher at Abilene Christian College for over thirty years, and because he can do a bit of everything he is presently maintaining a sixty-six unit apartment for retired persons.

We had the usual memorable papers that year. Jim Lee gave his latest take on how to test a fiancé or how to drive a wife to the point of violence in his paper, "Eating Over the Sink, and Other Marital Strategies." Kenneth Munson of San Marcos conducted a small-scale play party. Weiman Meinzer gave the banquet speech with a slide show and talk on coyotes, and reminded everybody of his favorite coyote story.

My coyote story was about a prize watermelon Grandad was raising to show off at the Abernethy reunion soon to come up on the Washita ranch. The watermelon patch was down the hill toward the river, about a quarter mile from the house. Every morning Grandad and I would go check the watermelon patch. We soon found that the coyotes could sense when a melon was ripe and would roll it over, bite through the yellowed underside, and gobble up its heart. We had lost several melons to coyotes, and Grandad decided that he had better take precautions with his Watt Long melon, so called because he had a large fat friend named Watt Long. So we ringed that prize melon with a dozen traps, so many I was almost scared to walk in the melon patch, afraid that they would jump over and snap me. The Watt Long was just coming in when one morning we made our inspection and found that the coyotes had gotten hold of the melon's vine, had dragged it out through the now-snapped traps, and had eaten a neat hole through the yellowing bottom. Grandad was so amused and amazed at the coyotes' skill and intelligence that he laughed and slapped his knee and said, "Well, I'll be doggone!" Grandad never got tired of telling the story about the smart coyotes.

And I remember my amazement when I saw my dog Pal walking paw on paw with a coyote through the Washita sand.

The publication for 1996 was *Juneteenth Texas: Essays in African-American Folklore* (PTFS 54–1996) I had sent out a message to contributors in a special letter mailed on August 22, 1994:

"The Texas Folklore Society has been publishing Southwestern folklore since 1912 and has been publishing multi-ethnic folklore ever since volume one. In 1991 the Society published *Hecho en Tejas*, a volume on Texas-Mexican folklore [PTFS 50–1991, Joe Graham, editor]. We now plan to publish a volume on Afro-American folklore in Texas. The publication is as yet unnamed (Midnight Special? East Dallas Special? Suggest something!) but should be on the bookstands by the end of 1995 or in the spring of 1996. . . .

"Concerning style: Please remember our audience for this publication. We are not writing for professional folklorists, social historians, or elite academicians. We are writing to a broad, general audience of educated laymen, *American Heritage* readers, who will switch channels on us if we belabor them with academic minutiae, technical jargon, and sesquipedalianisms. . . .

"We do sincerely thank you for getting involved in this project. We know that we cannot come close to including the full range of black folklore in Texas, but the Society is going to give it its best shot and you are the bullets."

Juneteenth Texas was edited by this editor, his student Patrick Mullen, Director of the Center for Folklore Studies at Ohio State University, and Pat's student Alan Govenar, Director of Documentary Arts, Inc., of Dallas. This choice of three generations of editors had the value of three different time perspectives on all racial questions that arose. This also posed a problem. As the elder, I grew up in a segregated society, became a desegregationist during my time in the service during WWII, and am still amazed and pleased at how far we have come in race relations since Brown vs. Topeka in 1954. Pat was my student when I taught at Lamar, and he matured during the first spasms of desegregation in the Fifties and Sixties and still bears the zeal and the guilt that seems to be a part of the early white activists of the integration movement. Alan of Boston, Massachusetts, was Pat's student at the

University of Texas in the 1970s. He grew up in an integrated society and had trouble understanding what the Southern world was like during segregation. Among the editorial remarks in the "Preface" are the following: "The editors and writers of *Juneteenth Texas* do not agree among ourselves about everything regarding the presentation and analysis of African-American culture, but we are all in agreement about the value of studying cultural differences as well as cultural similarities." (ix)

Juneteenth Texas did not come out in 1995, as it was supposed to, but it did make it handily for the 1996 PTFS. The building of it went slowly. The editors had problems among themselves dealing with racial issues. We had problems dealing with writers over racial issues—what words to use, differing attitudes about what happened in history, and what was fit for public consumption and what was not. We were constantly stepping into one cultural gap or another. But we did it, and I am proud that *Juneteenth Texas* is a Society book.

And it had one of the prettiest dust jackets ever to grace a PTFS. The burnt orange jacket features a painting of shotgun, row houses in Houston's Fourth Ward by John Biggers, one of my favorite artists and people.

Juneteenth Texas was recognized and showcased at the Texas Book Festival on November 15–16, 1996, with a special panel on black folklore. And I went sailing out to LA to tell the folks at the Gene Autry Museum all about Juneteenth. They already knew all about Juneteenth! An Arizona black lady in my audience said that they had celebrated Juneteenth in Tucson for years. And the next day's Sunday June 20th *Los Angeles Times* carried a story about Juneteenth that covered a third of the front page. The news story had nothing to do with my speech. Soon thereafter the House of Representatives passed a resolution recognizing Juneteenth. I guess that particular Texas holiday is going to become national eventually.

The University of North Texas Press produced 2,548 copies of *Juneteenth Texas* for $15,904.05.

Carolyn Fiedler Satterwhite, assistant editor and office secretary, was elected that year as the Society's treasurer. Even though Edwin Gaston of Nacogdoches had been, on my request, the nominal treasurer since 1971, Carolyn had been handling the finances ever since she took over the management of the TFS office. Electing Carolyn was a move to simplify Society bookkeeping. In 1996 Carolyn announced that the TFS balance was $145,252.92, a healthy number and proof that it takes money to make money.

Wyman Meinzer on "Coyotes!"

The Easter snow in Abilene

1997

Margaret Tate Waring
President 1996–97 at Huntsville
Founder and head of the Comanche Public Library, life member of the Texas State Historical Association, named Texas Library Association Small Community Librarian of the Year and Comanche Woman of the Year

For myself, I never could believe that Hong Kong would really be turned over to the Chinese, but the British did release it, amidst much mourning on the part of some and much righteous jubilation from the Chinese sympathizers. So far—now in 2000—not much has changed. My tattoo man, Jimmy Ho, said back in '86 that the Chinese would use Hong Kong to express all their latent capitalist inclinations. I have heard that the prices of food and hotels have increased considerably.

We met in Huntsville for the 1997 meeting, on the Sam Houston State University campus at its University Hotel. I am impressed with universities that have their own hotels. Easter weekend in 1997 fell on March 27–29, and Margaret Waring of Comanche presided. Margaret is a research historian as well as the Society's official Texas Librarian of the Year. Gene and Marynell Young and Melvin Mason arranged the meeting.

The members' annual for 1997 was a traditional miscellany entitled *Between the Cracks of History: Essays on Teaching and Illustrating Folklore* (PTFS 55–1997). *Between the Cracks* was a spin-off of the Society's pedagogical session at the Fort Worth meeting in 1995. A goodly number of the TFS members teach or have taught folklore in the public schools and universities. Teachers—and many Society members—take for granted that everybody can define, explain, and illustrate folklore. Unfortunately, as we can see from un-folklorish papers presented at meetings, not everybody has thought about the technicalities of folklore. For that reason we periodically have sessions on the nature of our discipline as a refresher course. *Between the Cracks* is one result of that refresher course, and hopefully it is used by teachers who want to get a better bead on what folklore is and how to teach it.

Fran and I decided on the *Between the Cracks* title while we were discussing the contents of this miscellany. We agreed that folklore consisted, in part, of information which fell between the cracks when historians, biologists, artists, etc. were pursuing their academic disciplines. Thus a chapter in a history book might discuss the East Texas oil boom of the 1930s but it will probably leave out Mattie's Palm Isle dance hall or what it was like living in an oil field camp. The folklorist will quickly fasten on to these latter items and get papers and publications out of them.

Between the Cracks cost $10,643.14 for 2,042 copies. In 1997 we also came out with second printings, this time in paperback, of Joe Graham's *Hecho en Tejas* (PTFS 50–1991) at $6,446.89 for 2,063 copies and *Texas Toys and Games* (PTFS 48–1989) at $6,643.07 for 2,037 copies. The Society's total assets in 1979 was $145,608.57, so we felt that we could afford to reprint, especially since a major purpose of the TFS is to publish and present Texas folklore.

In the Juneteenth 1997 newsletter is an editor's comment at the end of the listing of the Society's total assets: "My goal is to break $150,000 so that we can invest $100,000 and operate on $50,000. We're getting close."

In November 1997, I had a head-on collision with a drunk who was driving in my lane and was traumatically reminded of my mortality and obligations. Coincidentally, a month earlier, on October 3, 1997, I had written UNT Press Director Fran Vick the following letter involving my secretarial obligations:

"About the matter of TFS secretarial succession: ideally I would get somebody in here at SFA and pass the position and the office over to him or her. One reason that I would like to keep the Society on this campus is that every administration, from English department head through deans to the president, has supported the Society completely. I have asked for very little that I have not gotten. Whatever its future, the Society must have a supporting university base from which to operate. Also, I hate the thought of moving all the records and paper that I have accumulated since 1971. As to the latter, however, I hope to have all the records organized and turned in to the Barker Center with the rest of the TFS records by the end of 1998. But there is still a lot to move, when the time comes. Also, I think that Nacogdoches and SFA are a good headquarters, considering the historical nature of this area.

"I don't see the quittin' time coming immediately, but I do want to prepare for 'eventualities,' and you offered the best suggestion that I can think of. Yes, I would like for you to handle the TFS secretary-editorship in case of an emergency. You know more about the inner workings of the Society and its publication program than anybody else. And you probably have had more contact with all of its members than anybody else, except Carolyn. Between you and Carolyn you could put the Society on the international map. I will bring this up before the board at the 1998 meeting, and if anything happens between now and then, you can send the board members this letter."

The files were not turned in to the Barker Center in 1998. I am using the TFS files to write this volume three of the TFS history, and I have been organizing them for the archives as I go. Hopefully, when this volume is finished, the files will be in shape for depositing. I did bring this successor business before the directors in 1998, and they agreed that in the event of my demise or incapacitation Fran Vick would act as executor and temporary secretary-editor of the Society until a new director could be found (June 23, 1998, TFS Newsletter). When these plans were made public at the 1998 business meeting, they started a whole flurry of applications for the office. It is good to know that interested and qualified applicants are on hand.

1998

Rollo K. Newsom
President 1997–98 at Sherman
Chairman of the Department of Sociology, Dean of the College of General Studies, Vice President for Academic Affairs at Southwest Texas State University, taught courses in Folkways and Folklore, now Distinguished Professor of Sociology and Folklore Emeritus

So that you can keep this year from running into other years that were similar: This was the year that the Bill Clinton-Monica Lewinski affair dominated the news media and the year that the president was impeached but escaped fairly unscathed. And having nothing to do with the White House, Viagra appeared on druggists shelves to save mankind from the curse of impotence. And the two most potent baseball players were Mark McGwire and Sammy Sosa, who broke all the records for home runs, with Mark hitting seventy.

One of the better things that the Texas Folklore Society did in 1998 was to get from Bill Wittliff and Encino Press all of the books that he had left over and stored from the Society's Encino days. On our first visit to inspect these remains, Bill took Fran and me to the large dark and dusty garage behind Encino. That first visit was as depressing as what we had to pay to get them and then get them bound. Fran did return. She collected the bound and unbound volumes and then sent the usable volumes to be bound and made ready for sales.

Wittliff had boxes of six volumes, which we obtained. The books included *Tire Shrinker to Dragster* (PTFS 34–1967), Emma Wilson Emery's *Aunt Puss & Others* (PBS 3–1969), John Q. Anderson's

Texas Folk Medicine (PBS 5–1970), *Diamond Bessie & The Shepherds* (PTFS 36–1971), *What's Going On?* (PTFS 40–1976), and *Paisanos* (PTFS 41–1978).

Fran Vick paid Bill Wittliff $1,250 for the whole batch of books, many of which were unbound and unusable. The Society paid $11,550.99 for binding 3,691 books at an average of $3.23 per book. With this transaction, the Society and UNT Press gained control of all of the Society's books.

The Society—with the help of James Winfrey, Larry Warburton, and Sylvia Grider—completed its collection of first editions of all of the Society's publications. These included our regular publications as well as those that were special publications (Range Life Series and Paisano Books) or those that it used as Extra Books.

The 1998 Society book to members was a paperback reprint of *Texas Folk and Folklore* (PTFS 26–1954) with added illustrations and a new preface. The reprint was christened *The Best of Texas Folk and Folklore*: 1916–1954. (ExB–22, 1998). UNT Press printed 1500 copies for $6,341.26. The book sold for $18.95.

I sent this *The Best of* Extra Book with many misgivings. The members expect a new book annually and a hardback book. This was neither. But this was our most used PTFS for classroom study, in both high school and college, and it had been rare and out of print for several decades. Fran and I had received calls for the book over the last years. Also, most of the TFS members are post-1954 by several years and do not have *Texas Folk and Folklore* in their libraries. Fran and I decided that we had to reprint it, and because we did not have a book in press for '98, *The Best of* was the practical choice. We did get some static from members, as well we should. And we apologized and promised to do better.

Those first fifty years of the Society were the best years for collecting primary folklore, the best of which went into the 1954 anthology. Those old annuals were filled with real, field collected folklore, with stories and songs and superstitions that truly had been passed down traditionally, without benefit of printing press, radio, or television. Frank Dobie was responsible for collecting and encouraging collecting most of it. The Society had published twenty-five annuals by 1954, so Mody Boatright and Wilson M. Hudson, Mody's successor, pulled together the best from those years and published *Texas Folk and Folklore*. It became the textbook for Texas folklore studies and the best folklore anthology on the market. It still is, and hopefully the Society will publish a companion anthology to illustrate the best of Texas folklore studies for the second half of the twentieth century.

Rollo Newsom was the TFS president in 1998. Rollo, of singular eminence, was progressionally a professor, department chair, dean, and vice president at Southwest Texas State University. He called the eighty-second annual meeting to order on April 10 at the Holiday Inn in Sherman, Texas. Jerry Lincecum and wife Peggy Redshaw were our hosts.

At the business meeting the Board named Fran Vick as next in line should the secretary-editor make an unexpected exit. She became an ex officio member of the TFS Board of Directors.

Of the Societal concerns that came out of the Sherman meeting, several members voiced their objections to having academic papers presented at the banquet. They believed that they had had all the learned folklore that they could stand during the regular sessions of the day, and they asked for more entertaining fare after the rigors of a formal banquet. These were considerations for the future.

Jeff Gorvetzian came before the members at Sherman, requesting our endorsement of a monument for the spaceship that hit a windmill and crashed in Aurora, Texas, in 1897. The unearthly pilot had been buried in the Aurora Cemetery, and Jeff and friends were raising money to erect a new memorial headstone. Various board members walled their eyes and started backing up in the traces. These reservations—plus the fact that we never heard from him after the meeting—caused the board to put their money on some other badger fight.

Elmer Kelton, with Jerry Lincecum and Peggy Redshaw, hosts at Sherman

1999

Sylvia Gann Mahoney
President 1998–99 at Midland
Works as director of institutional advancement at Vernon Regional Junior College, former English instructor and rodeo coach at New Mexico Junior College, founder of Lea County Cowboy Hall of Fame and Western Heritage Center, freelance writer and photographer

The Texas Folklore Society entered 1999, the last year of this second millennium, with a treasury balance of $160,112.28. We had reached and surpassed our goal of $150,000, which would allow us $100,000 in investments and $50,000 to operate on. Compare that with the Society's working capital in 1974, which was $2,158.32. We are living in comfortable times. Enjoy them!

The Texas Folklore Society met for its Ninetieth Anniversary meeting on Easter weekend, April 1–3, 1999, at the Holiday Inn in Midland, Texas. The ladies ran that meeting and it was the most efficiently handled gathering in memory. Cowgirl Sylvia Mahoney, school teacher and rodeo coach in Vernon, was the president. Mary Harris of Hobbs, New Mexico, was program chairman and vice president. And Midland's Savage sisters, Cynthia and Sarana, were the local arrangers. Ah, if women could only run the world!

The Society and Paul Patterson celebrated ninetieth birthdays (1909 to 1999!) at the Midland meeting with a cake and candles and a fire warden to see that all that large a conflagration did not burn down the Holiday Inn. The Society looked back on its ninety years and saw that it—and Paul—was still strong in wind and limb. We have grown in ways far beyond our treasury. We have met annually and continually since 1909, except when interrupted by wartime. We have collected, presented, and preserved more folklore than any other similar society in the United States. We have amassed a list of publications in Texas folklore that compare favorably with if not surpass collections throughout the United States. We have brought in to Texas and sent out from Texas some of the leading folklorists of the nation. And large numbers of the Society's members continue to gather annually to honor and enjoy the traditions of Texas. The Society is a close-knit band of brothers and sisters, and we easily become emotional about the Society and each other. Part of that sentimentality is that we are all a little long in the tooth and very conscious of the passing and the ending of time. People with whom we have shared our lives become increasingly precious. The traditions of Texas that we have all loved and been a part of for so long become increasingly precious. The last bites become increasingly precious!

The Society had all sorts of coverage at the Midland meeting. The Savage Sisters had arranged for the entire meeting to be videotaped. AV Workshop Productions of Midland did the taping and sold the tapes to members for twenty-five dollars.

Additionally, Elaine Davenport of Writer's AudioShop in Austin made a commercial audiotape of ten of the papers and packaged it with a Michael Murphey introduction. The package contains two cassettes for 180 minutes and will be titled "The Best of Texas Folklore, 1999." The copyright will be in the name of the Texas Folklore Society, 2000, and the royalty to the Society will be eight to ten percent, depending on the number of tapes sold. The price has not been decided upon at this writing time.

The Sisters provided an extra attraction for members in a trip to the legendary Horsehead Crossing of the Pecos River. Patrick Dearen, who wrote *Crossing the Pecos*, was the guide and lecturer.

Rusty Hudelson and the Bum Steers of Levelland, a South Plains College "western" band, entertained the members after the banquet. They put on a fine show, playing music in the style of the old Sons of the Pioneers and the new Riders in the Sky.

The members' book for 1999 was *Features and Fillers: Texas Journalists on Texas Folklore* (PTFS 56–1999), edited by Jim Harris of Hobbs, New Mexico, and Assistant Editor Carolyn Satterwhite of this office. The Society claims many journalists in its midst, Jim

Harris being one of them, in addition to being an English professor. Most of the Society's journalists are of this "in addition" type, writing for newspapers and magazines as a sideline rather than as a vocation. The result, however, is that much of our popularly disseminated folklore is circulated through newspapers by folklorists. Jim went out among the Society's practicing folklorists—the Writers among us, found a large number who regularly wrote for newspapers, and gleaned the best of their writing for *Features and Fillers*. The book is a fitting finale for this century.

As 1999 progressed, dire predictions were abroad about the technological consequences of moving into a new century and millennium. We were warned that the Y2K bug, a bit of folklore itself, might possibly devour computer programs which control America's business and infrastructure, as well as this TFS office. Without computer guidance, some opined, electical systems for cities would fail, gas pressure would fall, and water systems would shut down. The bug would cause banks to collapse, and we would be without money. Citizens could, and some did, work themselves into a full-scale panic. They stored food and water, stashed money, and bought generators to carry them across the line into the new millennial time frame.

Equally dramatic, some sects talked pessimistically about Judgment Day and the end of the world. Others hoped for the Coming of Christ. Law enforcement panicked when an Algerian crossed the American-Canadian border with bombing supplies, and NYPD set up police protection against the New Year's bombing of Times Square. Happily, the crazies of the world stayed out of sight on December 31, 1999, and no riots or bombings were reported.

In fact, nothing out of the ordinary went amiss. Besides folks miswriting the new date on checks, life went on much as it had before we crossed the time line into 2000 A.D.

Americans watched television for twenty-four hours as citizens of the world celebrated the entrance of the New Millenium-Century-Year, starting in the Pacific islands and ending in the Pacific islands. France and the Eiffel Tower won the prize as the most splendid fireworks display of the twenty-four-hour show. London failed to fire up the Thames but did have a great smoke display. The cut-glass ball in Times Square fell, but not very dramatically. One of us drank a glass of champagne, kissed his near and dear, and went back to sleep. When he got up in this new time, he ate breakfast and looked outside. And the only thing that changed was that a stray cat was sleeping on his pickup.

Sylvia Mahoney, President; Cynthia Savage & Sarana Savage, Local Arrangers; Mary Harris, VP and Program Chairman at Midland in 1999

2000 A.D.

Mary R. Harris
President 1999–2000 at Nacogdoches
Assistant Professor of Education and Head of Special Education, College of the Southwest in Hobbs, taught school for thirty years, engineered and built solar-powered home

This is the first of January in the Third Millennium, which means that the January newsletter must soon be written and the invitation for the Easter meeting in Nacogdoches must be sent. Next week I shall write to the members that all is well in the TFS office and that we go into the new century with high hopes and great expectations. The Texas Folklore Society has crossed the boundary into the New Time, and so far, all that has happened has been good.

We will meet at the Fredonia Hotel in Nacogdoches on a late-Easter weekend, April 20–22, 2000. Mary Harris of the College of the Southwest at Hobbs, New Mexico, will preside. Jerry Lincecum of Austin College in Sherman will provide the program and the paper sessions look exciting. At the Friday night banquet the Secretary-Editor will pay tribute to the Society's office secretaries over the past twenty-nine years. Those present to receive their plaudits will be Martha Dickson (1971–1981), Carrol Daniels (1985–1989) and Carolyn Satterwhite (1989–present). The banquet entertainment will be provided by The East Texas String Ensemble of Nacogdoches.

Treasurer Carolyn Satterwhite will report that the Society's balance at the beginning of the year 2000 was $169,600.25. Editor Abernethy will report that the members' book for this year will be *The Texas Folklore Society: 1971–2000*, (PTFS 57–2000) volume III of the series, and that the book is presently at Fran Vick's University of North Texas Press but will be in members' hands this fall.

I shall report that Fran Vick and UNT Press is experimenting with a way to bring out-of-print books back in print through a new book distribution program by Lightning Print, Inc. LPI loads the out-of-print books into a database and can then electronically print books on demand to customers who order them. The books can be printed in about forty-eight hours. Lightning Books then ships the printed and bound book directly to the customer. TFS has nearly one hundred books in its management, so this will insure that all of the Society's books will remain continually available to the public. Lightning Books can now have all of the TFS books in print again.

The Board of Directors will report that the Society is working toward several goals. Necessary for Society survival is the recruitment of young folklorists and new writers and presenters. We need to bring in more minorities, blacks and Hispanics, in particular, and get them into the machinery of the meetings and publications. The Society needs closer ties to the academic people and institutions of Texas and Southwest. We need continual and statewide publicity about the projects that TFS members are working on. And we must think and work continually to keep our present members involved in all phases of the Society's activities.

Members will leave Nacogdoches entertained and educated by the meeting's folklore scholarship and happy in the friendship of this annual gathering. They will feel that they are a part of a Texas tradition that has great value because of its intrinsic merit and because of its venerability. And they will hope that they make the meeting in 2001—and on and on.

Meetings and Publications of the Texas Folklore Society 1990 to 2000

Seventy-fourth annual meeting, April 12–14, 1990, Kingsville, sponsored by Texas A & I University.

Officers

President: Al Lowman

Vice President: Kenneth Davis

Secretary-Editor: F.E. Abernethy

Treasurer: Edwin W. Gaston

General Counsel: William N. Stokes

Directors: Jim Harris, Faye Leeper, James C. McNutt, Sarah Greene, Lou Rodenberger

Councilors: Lora B. Garrison, Mary Harris, Lee Haile, Bill Brett, Tony Clark

Program

Thursday, April 12

Gala Premiere of "Come Hungry, Come Thirsty," a new documentary on camp meetings by Melvin Mason, Huntsville.

Hootenanny

Friday, April 13

Session I

Chair: John O. West

"Vaquero Folk Arts and Crafts Traditions in South Texas," Joe Graham, Kingsville

"The Roadside Cross Tradition in South Texas," Alberto Barrera, Kingsville

"The Tejano Yard Art Tradition on Starr County," Eric Ramos, Kingsville

"Religious Folk Art in the Robstown Tejano Community," Cynthia Vidauri, Kingsville

"Tejano Religious Folk Art in Rural South Texas Cemetaries," Chris Potter, Kingsville

Session II

Chair: Lou Rodenberger

"Community Gospel Singing," Richard Mason, Midland

"Folk Tales in the African-American Cultural Traditions," Lorece Williams and Early Teel, San Antonio

"Hammered Dulcimers and Folk Songs: The Musical Heritage of the C.A. Lee Family," Jean Granberry Schnitz, Boerne

"Hero Worship on the Drilling Rig: A Sense of Place," T.E. Breedlove

"Good Eating, Good Providing," Lera Lich, Waco

Session III

Chair: Jim Byrd

"A Tribute to Paul Patterson," Elmer Kelton, San Angelo

"Paul Patterson the Teacher," Ernestine Sewell, Commerce

"Narrative Technique in the Fiction of Paul Patterson," Lawrence Clayton, Abilene

"Printing the Poems of Paul Patterson Perfectly," Charles Linck, Commerce

Session IV

Chair: Mary Harris

"Folktales in a Time and Place," Dean Nichols, Dallas
"Personal Narratives About Snakes: An Emic Genre in North Central Texas," Linda Kinsey Adams, Bloomington, Indiana (Sweetwater, Texas)
"The Hot Tamale Man," Mrs. John Q. Anderson, Ruston, Louisiana
"Ghosts, Goblins, Virgins, and Other Supernatural Creatures," Michael Felker, Lubbock
"Lighter Moments in Medicine," Jeri Tanner, Lubbock
"The Lore of the Lush: Certain Rambling Observations on the Lore of the Bibulous Proclivities of Homo Sapiens," Ernest Speck, Alpine
Banquet: "Sin in Old Bell County, 1955–1959 or How I Got My Start in the Texas History 'Bidness'," Ron Tyler, Director, Texas State Historical Association
Session V
Chair: Dorys Grover
"Amanda and William Franklin Burks: A Nueces County Partnership," Johnye C. Sturcken
"Cavalry Traditions on the Texas Frontier," James T. Matthews, Lubbock
"A Cowboy Remembers," Mildred Boren, San Angelo
"By Their Pickups Ye Shall Know Them," Lon Shell, San Marcos
"Gilley's Gardol and Gomorrah: The Invisible Shield between Pasadena and Houston," Gretchen Lutz, Pasadena
Business meeting
Session VI
Chair: Margaret Waring
"Technology and the Modern Cowboy Tale," Rebecca Carnes, Lubbock
"Not Hobbling Their Lips: Cowboy Talk in the Campfire Tales of Andy Adams," Dick Heaberlin, San Marcos
"Humor in Modern Cowboy Poetry," Jim Harris, Hobbs, New Mexico
"Class von otto," Ellisene Davis, Keller
"Semana Santa in Antigua, Guatemala," Charles Martin, Denton

The Bounty of Texas. PTFS XLIX. Francis Edward Abernethy, editor. Denton: University of North Texas Press, 1990.

CONTENTS

Seventy-fifth annual meeting, March 28–30, 1991, San Marcos, hosted by Southwest Texas State University.
Officers
President: Kenneth W. Davis
Vice President: Jeri Tanner
Secretary-Editor: F.E. Abernethy
Treasurer: Edwin W. Gaston
General Counsel: William N. Stokes
Directors: Sarah Greene, Faye Leeper, Al Lowman, Lou Rodenberger, William N. Stokes
Councilors: Lora B. Garrison, Lee Haile, Mary Harris, Elmer Kelton, Margaret Waring
Program
Thursday March 28
Tours: San Marcos Historical Sites, Staples, Fentress Historical Sites
Reception: Southwestern Writer's Collection, University Library
Hootenanny
Friday, March 29
Session I
Chair: Joyce Roach, Keller
"Sunbonnets as Folk Costumes," Janet K. Jeffery, Austin
"Windshield Cowboy," L.H. Warburton, Jr., Alice
"Linguistic Innovation and Conservatism: Dialect in Cowboy Poetry," Mary Jane Hurst, Lubbock
Session II
Chair: Sarah Greene, Gilmer
"Beautifully Printed and Expressive of Texas: Carl Hertzog and the T.F.S.," Al Lowman, San Marcos
"College Creates a New Breed of Cowboy," Sylvia Mahoney, Vernon
"Laughing at the Clouds: Texas Drought Humor," Rana Williamson, Ft. Worth
"My Father's Home Towns: Family Saga and Sense of Place," Lou Rodenberber, Baird
Session III
Chair: Annette Milton, Dallas
"Vaquero: Where It All Began," John West, El Paso
"The Lost Chisos Mine," Patrick Dearen, Midland
"J. Frank Dobie, Mody Boatright, and me," James W. Winfrey, Houston
"Peripatetic Proselytizing," Julie Whitsitt, Lubbock

Session IV
Chair: Ann Miller, Waco
"Neglected Texas History," Charles Chupp, De Leon
"Forked Stick Folklore," George Ewing, Abilene
"The First Thing We Do, Let's Kill All the Lawyers," Phyllis Bridges, Denton
Banquet: Curt Brummett, Speaker
Saturday, March 30
Session V
Chairs: Arthur Hendrix, Commerce, and Elmer Kelton, San Angelo
"A Piece of Roast," Paul Patterson, Pecos
"Mountain Oysters, et al," James W. Byrd, Commerce, and Greg Hendrix, Temple
"Pie," James Ward Lee, Denton
"Dobie's Only Child: The Texas Folklore Society in 1926," F.E. Abernethy

Hecho en Tejas: Texas-Mexican Folk Arts and Crafts. PTFS L. Joe S. Graham, ed. F.E. Abernethy, general ed. Denton: University of North Texas Press, 1991

CONTENTS

Seventy-Sixth Annual Meeting, McKinney, April 16–18, 1992, sponsored by Collin County Community College, Center for Texas Studies, University of North Texas, University of North Texas Press
Officers
President: Jeri Tanner
Vice-President: Dick Heaberlin
Secretary-Editor: F.E. Abernethy
Treasurer: Edwin W. Gaston
Directors: Sarah Greene, Al Lowman, Faye Leeper, William N. Stokes, Kenneth W. Davis
Councilors: Lee Haile, Margaret Waring, Elmer Kelton, Frances B. Vick, B. W. Aston
Program
Thursday, April 16
Tours: Heritage Farmstead Museum, Plano; Bolin Wildlife Exhibit, McKinney
Hootenanny, Holiday Inn, McKinney
Friday, April 17
Session 1
Welcome by McKinney Mayor, John Gay
Chair: Richard Holland, San Marcos
"The Horsetrading Context: Suspended Ethics, Live-buying, and Boot," J. Rhett Rushing, Stanford, California
"You Have No Idea How Bad it Was: Dust Bowl Stories," Becky Carnes Matthews, Lubbock
"The Doan's Picnic," William N. Stokes, Jr., Dallas
Session 2
Chair: Joe S. Graham, Kingsville
"The Built Environment of Early Spanish, Mexican, and Mexican-American Ranches Along the Rio Grande," Joe S. Graham, Kingsville
"Early Mexican and Mexican-American Ranching Architecture in Jim Hogg and Duval Counties in South Texas," Alejandro Saenz, Kingsville
"Making and Building with Sillares (Caliche Blocks) in South Texas," Mary Anna Casstevens, Kingsville
"Early Chapels and Altars on Texas Mexican Ranches in South Texas," Cynthia L. Vidaurri, Kingsville
Session 3
Chair: Melvin Mason, Huntsville
"Who is Digging on my Grave? The Corps of Engineers?" Charles B. Martin, Denton
"No Eared Joe: Oil Field Folk Hero in a Time and Place," T.E. Breedlove, Jr., La Grange
"Motorcycles, Song Lyrics, Football and Majorettes: Grave Markers for Youth in Central Texas," Rollo Newsom, San Marcos
"Erich Riesel, Ironworker," Candace Leslie, Bryan
Session 4
Chair: John O. West, El Paso
"Folklore Influences in Contemporary Country Music," Walter Killam, Denton

"The Language of the Trail Drivers: An Examination of the Origin and Diffusion of an Industry-Oriented Vocabulary," W.C. Jameson, Conway, Arkansas
"Red Raiders for West Texas: The Development of a Tradition," Jim Matthews, Lubbock
"More Bullcorn About Folk-Say," Ernest B. Speck, Alpine
Banquet: "The Uses of Folklore," James Ward Lee, Denton
Saturday April 18
Session 5
Business meeting
Session 6
Chair: Joyce Roach, Keller
"Stinson Behlen, Dulcimer Maker," Kenneth W. Davis, Lubbock
"An East Texas Lynching: The Humphries/Wilkinson-Greenhaw Feud," Mark Busby, San Marcos
"Vamos Por Lena (Let's go for wood)," Jim Harris, Hobbs, New Mexico
"Abernethy Stew: Toward a Post Structural Analysis of Some of the Work of Francis E. Abernethy," Rosemary Killam, Denton
Tours: Old Post Office Museum

The Texas Folklore Society 1909–1943, Volume I. PTFS LI. Francis Edward Abernethy. Denton: University of North Texas Press, 1992.

CONTENTS

Seventy-Seventh Annual Meeting, San Angelo, April 8–10, 1993. Hosted by Angelo State University Department of English
Officers
President: Dick Heaberlin
Vice-president: Mildred Boren Sentell
Secretary-Editor: F.E. Abernethy
Treasurer: Edwin W. Gaston
Directors: Al Lowman, Faye Leeper, Bill Stokes, Kenneth W. Davis, Jeri Tanner
Councilors: Margaret Waring, Elmer Kelton, Fran Vick, B.W. Aston, J. Rhett Rushing
Program
Thursday, April 8

Tours of Ft. Concho
Hootenanny
Friday, April 9
Session I
Chair: Margaret Waring, Comanche
"Pobre Ricardo's Almanac," John O. West, El Paso
"Penitentiary Slang," Albert Campbell, Bryan
"Is That Your Name, or a Nickname," Dean P. Nichols, Dallas
"Gidget Goes to Acuna," Becky Cornell, San Angelo
Session II
Chair: Betty Alldredge, San Angelo
"Meaner Than Hell But All Locked Up," Kenneth W. Davis, Lubbock
"Where Have You Been, Billie Sol, Billie Sol," Delight Roach, Dallas
"Last of the Frontier," L.H. Warburton, Alice
"Thomas V. Skaggs," Beverly Six Case, Alpine
Session III
Chair: Diane Christian, San Angelo
"From Sparking to Happily Ever After," Margaret Cox, Austin
"A Menard Childhood," Rana K. Williamson, Fort Worth
"Enduring the Depression Years," Maisie Paulissen, Houston
"Punching Sticks and Flannel Wrapped Bricks," Ernestine Sewell Linck, Commerce
Session IV
Chair: Ira Blanton, Alpine
"Making, Carving, and Playing Musical Instruments," Judith Hakes, San Angelo
"Folks Doodle," George Ewing, Abilene
"The Oilfield Camp," James W. Winfrey, Houston
"Folk Use of Mnemonics," Jerry Crouser, San Angelo
Reception, Ft. Concho
Banquet, "Holier Than Thou," Joyce Roach and Bob Flynn, speakers
Saturday, April 10
Business meeting
Session V
Chair: Kenneth Davis, Lubbock
"Looseherding the Truth," Ira Blanton, Alpine
"Bluebird Mare from Sterling City," Patrick Dearen, Midland
"Roughstring Rider," Jack Douglas, Littlefield
Session VI
Chair: Gloria Duarte Valverde, San Angelo
"Thaipusam," Robert Mitchell, Bandera
"Lost Souls, Ghost Stories," Brian Bethel, San Angelo
"The Night the Stars Fell," Robert Duncan, McKinney

Corners of Texas. PTFS LII. Francis Edward Abernethy, editor. Denton: University of North Texas Press, 1993.

CONTENTS

Seventy-Eighth Annual Meeting, Victoria, March 31 through April 2, 1994, held at Holiday Inn, hosted by Victoria College

Officers

President: Mildred Boren Sentell

Vice President: Faye Leeper

Secretary-Editor: F. E. Abernethy

Treasurer: Edwin W. Gaston

Councilors: Fran Vick, B. W. Aston, J. Rhett Rushing, Phyllis Bridges, Sylvia Mahoney

Directors: Kenneth W. Davis, Jeri Tanner, Margaret Waring, Dick Heaberlin, George Ewing

Thursday, March 31

Registration
Walking Tour of historic downtown Victoria
Workshop: "Collecting Family Folklore" Rhett Rushing
Hootenanny
Program
Friday, April 1
Welcome: Dr. Jimmy L. Goodson, President of Victoria College and Victoria Chamber of Commerce
Session 1
Chairman: Ernestine Sewell, Commerce
"Names of Springs in Texas," Dick Heaberlin, San Marcos
"Bootlegging in Spring Texas," Elizabeth Kessler, Huntsville
"Herbs and Proverbs: Cures for Hurts and Hell," Sarana Savage and Cynthia Savage, Midland
"Spanish Gypsy Wedding," Charles Martin, Denton
Session 2
Chairman: Jim Harris, Hobbs, New Mexico
"Urban Lore" — Panel Discussion, John O. West, El Paso, Jim McNutt, San Antonio, Jo Lyday, Houston, Judy Alter, Fort Worth
Officers Luncheon
Session 3
Chairman: Jack Duncan, McKinney
"Folk Speech of the Contemporary Cowboy," Lawrence Clayton, Abilene
"How Do We Know the Bad Guys," Olivia Nichols, Dallas
"Three Days in November," Loraine Anderson, Ruston, LA
"Rituals of Police Burial," Phyllis Bridges, Denton
Session 4
Chairman: Lou Rodenberger, Abilene
"High Tech Lore," Kenneth Davis, Lubbock
"Victoria Won World War II," Jean Schnitz, Boerne
"Cedar Choppers," Ross McSwain, San Angelo
Reception at McNamara House Museum
Banquet: Biscuits O'Brien (Rev. Monte Jones), Speaker
Saturday, April 2
Session 5
Chairman: Joyce Roach, Keller
"Working with Martha Mitchell: A Reminiscence," Melvin Mason, Huntsville
"Remedies 1864," Jerry Lincecum, Sherman
Business Meeting
"Play Parties," Kenneth Munson, San Marcos
"Grease," James Ward Lee, Denton
Guided Tour, Presidio La Bahia, Goliad, Texas

The Texas Folklore Society 1943–1971. Volume II. PTFS LIII. Francis Edward Abernethy. Denton: University of North Texas Press, 1994.

CONTENTS

Seventy-Ninth Annual Meeting, April 13–15, 1995, Forth Worth. Green Oaks Inn
Officers
President: Faye Leeper
Vice President: George Ewing
Secretary-Editor: F. E. Abernethy
Treasurer: Edwin W. Gaston
Directors: Jeri Tanner, Margaret Waring, Dick Heaberlin, Mildred Sentell, B. W. Aston
Councilors: J. Rhett Rushing, Phyllis Bridges, Sylvia Mahoney, Georgia Caraway, R. G. Dean
Program:
Thursday, April 13
Hootenanny & Autograph party
Friday, April 14
Session 1
Chairman: Margaret Waring, Comanche
"Folklore of the Guadalupe Mountains," W. C. Jameson, Conway, Arkansas
"Little Joe the Wrangler," James W. Winfrey, Houston
"Repo Man," John Lightfoot, Lake Jackson
"Lore, Legends, Lies, and Bits of Truth about Coffee," Ernestine Sewell Linck, Commerce
Session 2
Chairman: F. E. Abernethy, Nacogdoches
"How I Define Folklore for My Students," Panel Discussion, James Byrd, Commerce, Joe Graham, Kingsville, Joyce Gibson Roach, Keller, Rhett Rushing, Bloomington, Indiana
Officers Luncheon
Session 3
Chairman: Ken Davis, Lubbock
"Weather-Nature Says," L. H. Warburton, Jr., Alice
"Gangs and Graffiti," Ken Untiedt, Lubbock
"Mothers, Bikers, and Time: Prison Art at the Old Bexar County Jail," Ansen Seale, San Antonio
"Sticks, Stones and What-Have-You: Contemporary Folk Gravemarkers," Rollo K. Newsom, San Marcos
Session 4
Chairman: Jerry Lincecum, Sherman

"Ed Bell, Teller of Tall Tales," Henry Wolff, Jr., Victoria
"It Began in a Wheelbarrow," David LaRo, San Anronio
"The Life of J. Mason Brewer, Black Folklorist," Jeri Tanner, Lubbock, and James W. Byrd, Commerce
Banquet, Ken Davis, Speaker, "Folkloristics and Fun: The Texas Style"
Saturday, April 15
Session 5
Chairman: Elizabeth Kessler, Spring
"Horse Hunting and My First Rodeo," Dorris Tull, Abilene
"Modern Small Town Rodeo Lore," Suzy Schoener Burnham, McKinney
Business Meeting
"College Cowgirls: From Queen to Contestant to Coach," Sylvia Gann Mahoney
"Fearlore: Fighting Dirty with Urban Legends," Rhett Rushing, Bloomington, Indiana

Eightieth Annual Meeting, Abilene, April 4–6, 1996, Embassy Suites Hotel
Officers
President: George Ewing
Vice President: Margaret Waring
Secretary-Editor: F. E. Abernethy
Treasurer: Edwin W. Gaston
Directors: Dick Heaberlin, Mildred Sentell, B. W. Aston, Faye Leeper
Councilors: Phyllis Bridges, Sylvia Mahoney, Georgia Caraway, R. G. Dean, Rollo Newsom
Program
Thursday, April 4
Hootenanny
Friday, April 5
Session 1
Chairman: Mary Harris, Hobbs, New Mexico
"The Legend of Jennie," Mary Joe Clendenin, Stephenville
"Massacre and Treasure on the Pecos," Patrick Dearen, Midland
"Water Woes and Water Ways, Tales of John B. Hawley, A Texas Engineer," Deborah Lightfoot Sizemore, Crowley
"Rail Tales, Some are True," Charles K. Oden, Austin
Session 2
Chairman: Jerry E. Hunt, Arlington
"The Devil Made Me Do It," Olivia Murray Nichols, Dallas
"Texans Say the Strangest Things," Theresa Flowers, Denton
"Back in the Saddle Again, Riding the Chrome-moly Horse," Lucille Enix, Dallas
Officers Luncheon
Session 3
Chairman: Lou H. Rodenberger, Baird
"Eating Over the Sink and Other Marital Strategies: A Guide for Redneck Husbands," James Ward Lee, Denton
"Cyclone Davis, Jr., A Texas Political Visionary," Gene Fowler, Austin

"School Yearbooks—Time Capsules of Texas Folklore," Jean Granberry Schnitz, Boerne
"The Trials and Tribulations of a West Texas Dirt Road Doctor," Mildred Boren Sentell, Snyder
Session 4
Chairman: Richard Holland, San Marcos
"Folklore and Cinema," Jim Harris, Hobbs, New Mexico
"Are Women 'Pushed Around' on Texas Dance Floors?" Betty Casey, Denton
"Prairie Nights to Neon Lights," Alan Munde and Joe Carr, Levelland
Banquet: "The Coyote in Southwestern Folklore," Wyman Meinzer, speaker
Saturday, April 6
Session 5
Chairman, Ira Blanton, Alpine
"Following the Footprints: Family Stories vs History," J. P. Brannen, Albuquerque, New Mexico
"A Family Legend: Gideon Lincecum and 'Killiecrankie,'" Jerry B. Lincecum, Sherman
Business Meeting
"Harley Sadler, The Texas Tent Show Man Extraordinaire," J. G. "Paw Paw" Pinkerton, Stamford, Connecticut

Juneteenth Texas: Essays in African-American Folklore. PTFS LIV. Francis E. Abernethy, Patrick B. Mullen, Alan B. Govenar, Editors. Denton: University of North Texas Press, 1996.

CONTENTS

Eighty-First Annual Meeting. Huntsville, March 27–29, 1997. Sam Houston State University.

Officers

President: Margaret Waring, Comanche

Vice President: Rollo K. Newsom, Austin

Secretary-Editor: F. E. Abernethy, Nacogdoches

Treasurer: Carolyn Satterwhite, Nacogdoches

Directors: B. W. Aston, Abilene; Mildred Sentell, Snyder; Faye Leeper, Irving; George Ewing, Abilene

Councilors: Georgia Caraway, Denton; R. G. Dean, Nacogdoches; Ira Blanton, Alpine; Tom Crum, Granbury; W. C. Jameson, Conway, Arkansas

Program

Thursday, March 27

Hootenanny

Friday, March 28

Session 1

Chairman: John Lightfoot, Lake Jackson

"The St. Joseph's Sausage Festival at Slaton, Texas: Communal Folk Gathering," Kenneth Davis, Lubbock

"This story has no lede (cq)!" Mike Cox, Austin

"Battles as Creation Epics: A Comparison of Texas's Alamo and Scotland's Culloden," Sylvia Grider, College Station

"Hawklore," Mary Harris, Hobbs, New Mexico

Session 2

Chairman: R. G. Dean, Nacogdoches

"Modern Epitaphs in Pictures and Words," Tom Breedlove, La Grange

"Cemetery Crawling in the State Capitol: Austin's Historic Cemeteries," L. Patrick Hughes (Austin)

"Life and Death in Old Bexar," David LaRo, San Antonio

"Buried in Texas Any and Every Which Way," Henry Wolff, Jr., Victoria

Officers Luncheon

Session 3

Chairman: Joe Moore, Wimberley

"Silva by Silva: A Life in Texas, 1902–1997," Silva Boze Brown (Commerce)

"Cow Pies and Politics," Jerry Nobles, Kirbyville
"Drought, Cut Worms, Sparrows and Little Green Sucking Lice," Pat Reese, Fort Worth
"Duval County—The Mesquite Curtain," L. H. Warburton, Jr., Alice
Session 4
Chairman: Rosemary Killam
"Catfishing: More Fib Than Fish," Rhett Rushing, Bloomington, Indiana
"Dancing Before the Altar: The Seises of Seville's Cathedral," Charles B. Martin, Denton
"'It All Began the Day My Conscience Died': Cheatin' Songs from Prototype to Postmodern," Dick Holland, Austin
Banquet, Speaker: Leon C. Metz, El Paso, "Chasing Gunfighters Across the Southwest"
Saturday, March 29
Session 5
Chairman: Jean Schnitz, Leon Springs
"Stick Cutting and Handling: An Ancient Folkway Lives on in Abilene," George Ewing, Abilene
Business Meeting
"How Cloth was Dyed During the Civil War in Washington County, Texas," Peggy A. Redshaw, Sherman
"Elmer Kelton and Allen Bosworth: Two Texans Who Know the Paisanos," John O. West, El Paso
Closing Ceremony

Between the Cracks of History: Essays on Teaching and Illustrating Folklore. PTFS LV. Francis E. Abernethy, editor. Denton: University of North Texas Press, 1997.

CONTENTS

Eighty-Second Annual Meeting. Sherman, April 9–11, 1998. Austin College, meeting host
Officers
President: Rollo Newsom
Vice President: Sylvia Mahoney
Secretary-Editor: F. E Abernethy
Treasurer: Carolyn Satterwhite
Directors: Faye Leeper, Irving; George Ewing, Abilene; Margaret Waring, Comanche; R. G. Dean, Nacogdoches
Councilors: Ira Blanton, Alpine; Tom Crum, Granbury; W. C. Jameson, Conway, Arkansas; Henry Wolff, Jr., Victoria; Mary Harris, Hobbs, New Mexico
Program
Thursday, April 9
Hootenanny
Friday, April 10
Session 1
Chairman: Joe Moore, Canyon Lake
"The Roy Bedichek Family Letters: Some Views on Doctors, Cures and Animal Life," Frances B. Vick, Denton
"The Founding and Traditions of the Sacred Heart Catholic Church in Rockne, Texas," Patrick Brannen Vick, Dallas
"The Roswell Incident—50th Anniversary Sell-Abration," Becky Matthews, Carlsbad, New Mexico
Session 2
Chairman: Cynthia Savage, Midland
"Echoes of Hope and Hebron—The Songs of Amos and Minnie Granberry," Jean Granberry Schnitz, Boerne
"Snakelore," F. E. Abernethy, Nacogdoches
"Take Me Out to the Ballgame," John Lightfoot, Lake Jackson
Session 3
Chairman: Jim Harris, Hobbs, New Mexico
"Boots, Hats, Grass, and Songs: Some Kansas Contributions to the Creation of the American Cowboy," Jim Hoy, Emporia, Kansas

"Horse of a Different Kind," Joy J. Burwell and Robert J. Duncan, McKinney
"The Police Language: The Lore of Law Enforcement Communication in West Texas," Ken Untiedt, Lubbock
Session 4
Chairman: Dick Holland, Austin
"Bound for Glory," Robert Flynn, San Antonio
"A Lesson to Last a Lifetime," J. G. "Paw-Paw" Pinkerton, Stamford, Conn.
"Roping the Wind: Cowboy Weather Lore of the Early Twentieth Century," Patrick Dearen, Midland
Banquet: Speaker, Stephen L. Hardin, "The Congressman, The Coonskin Cap, and the Creation of a Ring-tailed Roarer"
Saturday, April 11
Session 5
Chairman: Tom Crum, Granbury
"That'll be the Day: Festivals in Texas," Olivia Murray Nichols, Dallas
Business Meeting
"The Barrow Gang: Ralph Fults and His Years with Bonnie and Clyde," Melinda Williams, Denton
"Growing Up Female in Texas: The Importance of Beauty Pageants," Kelly Mosel, Austin
Closing Ceremony

Eighty-Third Annual Meeting, Midland, April 1–3, 1999, Holiday Inn
Officers
President: Sylvia Mahoney
Vice President: Mary Harris
Secretary-Editor: F. E. Abernethy
Treasurer: Carolyn Satterwhite
Directors: George Ewing, Margaret Waring, R. G. Dean, Rollo Newsom, Jerry Lincecum
Councilors: Ira Blanton, Tom Crum, W. C. Jameson, Henry Wolff, Jr.
Program
Thursday, April 1
Hootenanny & birthday celebration for Paul Patterson
Friday, April 2
Session 1, Chair: Karen Haile, Bandera
"Women A-Horseback, Side or Astride," Carolyn Norgaard, Dallas
"Extracts, Spices, and Soothing Ointments: Peddlers in Central Texas in the Thirties and Forties," Kenneth Davis, Lubbock
"History or Hearsay: Some Dubious Assertions about Bat Masterson and Bob Ford," Tony Clark, Georgetown
Session 2, Chair: John O. West, El Paso
"Survival Value in Fannin County, Texas: Then and Now," Wildwood Dean Price, Bonham
"Technology and Fast Foods Can Speed up the Aging Process," Faye Leeper, Irving
"La Charreada: The Traditions and Folklore of the Mexican Rodeo," Julia Kumor Hambric, El Paso

Session 3, Chair: Linda Clark, Georgetown
"The Oatmeal Festival: Folkways, Inventedways and Fakeways," Rollo Newsom, San Marcos
"Mother's Model T," George Ewing, Abilene
"Funeral Homes in Small West Texas Towns in the Early Part of the Century," Mildred Sentell, Snyder
Session 4, Chair: Jim Byrd, Commerce
"Talking Fancy," Jim Lee, Denton
"Somewhere Over the Pecos: A Patterson Oz," Patrick Dearen, Midland
"Paul Patterson: Teacher, Mentor, Friend," Elmer Kelton, San Angelo
Banquet: Sylvia Mahoney, presiding. Entertainment: Rusty Hudelson and "The Bum Steers" from South Plains College
Saturday, April 3
Session 5, Chair: Lee Haile, Bandera
"La Quinceanera: Hispanic Folk Custom," Phyllis Bridges, Denton
"Ghosts of Goliad," Henry Wolff, Jr., Victoria
Business Meeting
"Baby Lore: The Why and Wherefore of It," Joyce Roach, Keller
"Grandmother Lore: The Deep and Wide of It," Hazel Abernethy, Nacogdoches
"The High, Low and More of it," Audience participation
Closing Ceremony

Features and Fillers: Texas Journalists on Texas Folklore. PTFS LVI. Jim Harris, editor. Denton: University of North Texas Press, 1999.

CONTENTS

Eighty-Fourth Annual Meeting, Nacogdoches, April 20–22, 2000, Fredonia Hotel
Officers
President: Mary Harris
Vice President: Jerry Lincecum
Secretary-Editor: F. E. Abernethy
Treasurer: Carolyn Satterwhite
Counselor: William N. Stokes
Directors: Margaret Waring, R. G. Dean, Rollo Newsom, Sylvia Mahoney, John Lightfoot

Councilors: Henry Wolff, Jr., Tom Breedlove, Cynthia Savage, Jean G. Schnitz, Kenneth L. Untiedt
Program
Thursday, April 20
8:00 p.m. Hootenanny
Friday, April 21
Session 1
Chair: Fran Vick, Dallas
Welcome: TFS President–Mary Harris, Hobbs New Mexico
"Folklore by Osmosis: Three Decades with John O.," Lucy Fischer West, El Paso
"Now You Hear My Horn: Uses of the Blowing Horn in the Southern Big Woods Lifeway," Thad Sitton, Austin
"Violence in the Diamond of Texas," Larry Warburton, Alice
Session 2
Chair: Rollo Newsom, San Marcos
"The Making of a Househusband," Archie McDonald, Nacogdoches
"Grampa's Passion: Baseball," Linda Majors Clark, Georgetown
"Just Pain Mean: Louis T. Wigfall," Dallas Cothrum, Tyler
Noon: Officers luncheon
Session 3
Chair: Phyllis Bridges, Denton
"The Great Imposter Comes to Texas," Jerry Turner, Mt. Calm
"E-lore, or Even if You Don't Read This Please Forward it to Everyone You Know," Becky Matthews, San Antonio
"Seeing Red over Varsity Blues," Ty Cashion, Huntsville
Session 4
Chair: Peggy A. Redshaw, Sherman
"The Cottonseed Oil Mill," James Winfrey, Houston
"Chasing Virgins: Miraculous Images of Mary and Jesus in South Texas," J. Rhett Rushing, San Antonio
"Texas Tombstone Inscriptions," Nita Thurman, Dallas
Cash bar: 6:30 p.m.
Banquet: 7:30 p.m. Presiding: Mary Harris, Hobbs, New Mexico
Entertainment: East Texas String Ensemble
Saturday, April 22
Session 5
Chair: Sylvia Mahoney, Vernon
"New and Recycled Songs about Texas," Jean Schnitz, Boerne
"Pioneer Angel: Uncle Gus Wilson," Jack Duncan, McKinney, & Joy J. Burwell, Dayton
Business Meeting
"Robert Earl Keen: Texas Folk Traditions in Popular Music," Ken Untiedt, Lubbock, and Lee Haile, Bandera
Closing Ceremony

William N. Stokes, Legal Counselor and a generous friend of the Society

James W. Winfrey (at right)—Society benefactor, student of Frank Dobie, joined the Society in 1934—with wife Frances and Roger Garrison

Hazel Abernethy and Paul Patterson at the shrine of Don Pedrito Jaramillo, The Healer of Los Olmos, near Kingsville, 1989

Members do a line dance as a conjunto band played for a TFS baile after the Friday night banquet at Kingsville.

Joe Graham was the host for the 1990 meeting in Kingsville and the editor and author of the Golden Anniversary PTFS 50, *Hecho en Tejas: Texas-Mexican Folk Arts and Crafts*. At that time, Joe was a professor and Research Associate with the John E. Conner Museum at Texas A&I. Joe's education in folklore was directed by some of the Society's brightest lights: Sid Cox and John Q. Anderson at A&M, John O. West at UTEP, and Américo Paredes at UT. He was Folklorist in Residence at the Institute of Texan Cultures and spent a year of folklore fieldwork with a grant from the Texas Committee for the Humanities. Joe was born and raised in ranch life in the Big Bend, so his major work, *El Rancho in South Texas* (1994), was a natural result of his life and his learning. Joe is a very special person in the Society.

Joe Graham doing a Mexican boogie

Janell Whitt Chesnut

W. C. Jameson

Tom Crum

R. G. Dean

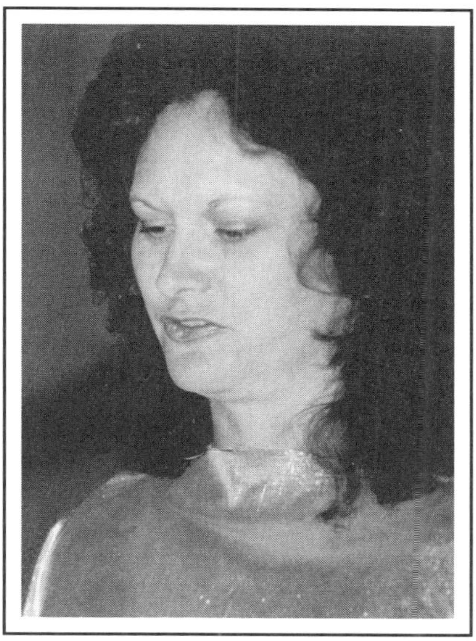

Becky Matthews

Charlie Oden

Tom Crum, Jim Byrd, Ken Davis, Elmer Kelton, Paul Patterson

Jasper and Marjorie Wright

Patrick Vick

Phyllis Bridges, Loraine Anderson, Jack Duncan, and Lawrence Clayton

Ross Vick, Ken Untiedt, and Kenneth Davis

Rhett Rushing

Lu Mitchell

Chester & Maureen Spaw

Tom Breedlove

Elizabeth Duncan and John O. West

J. G. Finkerton

Larry Warburton

The Haile sisters

Charles & Darlyn Martin, Paul Patterson, Elmer Kelton, Hazel Abernethy

Presidents of the Texas Folklore Society

(And Place Of Meeting At Which They Presided)

1909–11 Leonidas W. Payne, UT Austin (Austin)
1911–12 Theo. G. Lemmon, Dallas (Austin)
1912–13 Robert Adger Law, UT Austin (Austin)
1913–14 W.H. Thomas, A&M, College Station (Austin)
1914–15 Dorothy Scarborough, Baylor, Waco (Waco)
1915–16 Dr. Clyde Chew Glascock, Rice, Houston (Austin)
1916–17 Mrs. Lillie T. Shaver, Southwest Texas, San Marcos (San Marcos)
1921–22 Dr. Clyde Chew Glascock, Rice, Houston (Austin)
1922–23 Prof. Will H. Thomas, A&M, College Station (Austin)
1923–24 Julia Estill, Fredericksburg (Austin)
1924–25 Victor J. Smith, Sul Ross, Alpine (Austin)
1925–26 Prof. R.C. Harrison, Texas Tech, Lubbock (Austin)
1926–27 Prof. Gates Thomas, Southwest Texas, San Marcos (Austin)
1927–28 Col. M.L. Crimmins, Fort Sam Houston, San Antonio (Austin)
1928–29 Newton Gaines, TCU, Fort Worth (Fort Worth)
1929–30 John K. Strecker, Baylor, Waco (Austin)
1930–31 Jovita González, St. Mary's Hall, San Antonio (San Antonio)
1931–32 Jovita González, St. Mary's Hall, San Antonio (Austin)
1932–33 John K. Strecker, Baylor, Waco (Waco)
1933–34 Frost Woodhull, San Antonio (Austin)
1934–35 John Lee Brooks, SMU, Dallas (Dallas)
1935–36 Martha Emmons, State Home, Waco (Austin)
1936–37 Mabel Major, Fort Worth (Fort Worth)
1937–38 Charles L. Sonnichsen, TX School of Mines, El Paso (El Paso)
1938–39 R. A. Tsanoff, Rice, Houston (Houston)
1939–40 William A. Philpott, Dallas (Austin)
1940–41 John A. Lomax, Dallas (San Antonio)
1941–42 John A. Lomax, Dallas (Denton)
1942–43 Mody C. Boatright, UT Austin (Austin)
1943–44 Henry Nash Smith, UT Austin (No meeting in '44 & '45)
1944–45 Henry Nash Smith, UT Austin
1945–46 Frank Goodwyn, UT Austin (Austin)
1946–47 Brownie McNeil, TX A & I, Kingsville (Corpus Christi)
1947–48 Brownie McNeil, TX A & I, Kingsville (Austin)

1948–49 Brownie McNeil, TX A & I, Kingsville (San Antonio)
1949–50 John Lee Brooks, SMU, Dallas (Dallas)
1950–51 John Lee Brooks, SMU, Dallas (Austin)
1951–52 Haldeen Braddy, Texas Western, EL Paso (El Paso)
1952–53 Haldeen Braddy, Texas Western, El Paso (Austin)
1953–54 George Hendricks, North Texas, Denton (Denton)
1954–55 Elton R. Miles, Sul Ross, Alpine (Austin)
1955–56 John Q. Anderson, A&M, College Station (College Station)
1956–57 Hermes Nye, Dallas (Dallas)
1957–58 Wilson Hudson, UT Austin (Alpine)
1958–59 E. Hudson Long, Baylor, Waco (Austin)
1959–60 Martin Shockley, North Texas, Denton (San Antonio)
1960–61 Everett Gillis, Texas Tech, Lubbock (Austin)
1961–62 Américo Paredes, UT Austin (Monahans)
1962–63 Elizabeth Brandon, U of H, Houston (Austin)
1963–64 Edwin W. Gaston, Jr., Stephen F. Austin, Nacogdoches (Houston)
1964–65 Francis E. Abernethy, Lamar, Beaumont (Austin)
1965–66 James W. Byrd, East Texas, Commerce (Austin)
1966–67 Paul Patterson, Crane (Nacogdoches)
1967–68 James W. Lee, North Texas, Denton (Alpine)
1968–69 John O. West, UT El Paso (Dallas)
1969–70 Martha Emmons, Baylor, Waco (WImberley)
1970–71 Ralph Houston, Southwest Texas, San Marcos (San Antonio)
1971–72 Bessie M. Pearce, San Antonio College, San Antonio (College Station)
1972–73 Sid Cox, A&M, College Statio (Laredo)
1973–74 Orlan Sawey, TX A & I, Kingsville (Abilene)
1974–75 Ernest Speck, Sul Ross, Alpine (Houston)
1975–76 Joyce Roach, Keller (Arlington)
1976–77 Wm. H. Hardin, Houston (El Paso)
1977–78 Ernestine Sewell, Arlington (Nacogdoches)
1978–79 James M. Day, El Paso (Waco)
1979–80 Robert J. Duncan, McKinney (San Antonio)
1980–81 Lawrence Clayton, HSU, Abilene (Denton)
1981–82 Charles Martin, North Texas, Denton (Fredericksburg)
1982–83 Sylvia Grider, A&M, College Station (College Station)
1983–84 Charles Linck, ETSU, Commerce (Huntsville)
1984–85 Joe Graham, Millican (Abilene)
1985–86 Melvin Mason, Sam Houston SU, Huntsville (Jefferson)
1986–87 Jim Harris, Hobbs (Galveston)
1987–88 Lou Rodenberger, Baird (Lubbock)
1988–89 Sarah Greene, Gilmer (Uvalde)
1989–90 Al Lowman, San Marcos (Kingsville)
1990–91 Kenneth Davis, Texas Tech, Lubbock (San Marcos)
1991–92 Jeri Tanner, Texas Tech, Lubbock (McKinney)
1992–93 Dick Heaberlin, Southwest Texas, San Marcos (San Angelo)
1993–94 Mildred Boren Sentell, Snyder (Victoria)
1994–95 Faye Leeper, Irving (Fort Worth)

1995–96 George Ewing, Abilene (Abilene)
1996–97 Margaret Waring, Comanche (Huntsville)
1997–98 Rollo Newsom, Austin, Southwest Texas (Sherman)
1998–99 Sylvia Mahoney, Vernon (Midland)
1999–00 Mary Harris, Hobbs, New Mexico (Nacogdoches)

Boatright's Bodark, the gavel and knocker block made by Joseph Jones in 1979, passing from presidents Rollo Newsom to Sylvia Mahoney in 1998

James T. Bratcher, the maker of the *Analytical Index to Publications of the Texas Folklore Society, Volumes 1-36.* The Index was Bratcher's 1972 Ph.D. dissertation at the University of Texas, directed by Wilson M. Hudson, then Secretary-Editor of the Texas Folklore Society.

Chronological Listing of Publications of the Texas Folklore Society

[P=pamphlet; PTFS=numbered annual volume; ExB=extra book; RLS=Range Life Series; PBS=Paisano Book Series; SRP=special reference publication: Listing taken from Herbert C. Arbuckle's "Chronological and Bibliographical Listings of Texas Folklore Society Publications," *T for Texas: A State Full of Folklore* (PTFS XLIV, 1982)]

1	P-1	1912	*Some Current Folk-Songs of the Negro*. W.H. Thomas
2	PTFS-1	1916	*Round the Levee*. Stith Thompson, ed.
3	PTFS-2	1923	*Coffee in the Gourd*. J. Frank Dobie, ed.
4	PTFS-3	1924	*Legends of Texas*. Dobie, ed.
5	PTFS-4	1925	*Happy Hunting Ground*. Dobie, ed.
6	PTFS-5	1926	*Rainbow in the Morning*. Dobie, ed.
7	PTFS-6	1927	*Texas and Southwestern Lore*. Dobie, ed.
8	PTFS-7	1928	*Follow de Drinkin' Gou'd*. Dobie, ed.
9	ExB-1	1930	*Coronado's Children*. J. Frank Dobie
10	PTFS-8	1930	*Man, Bird and Beast*. Dobie, ed.
11	PTFS-9	1931	*Southwestern Lore*. Dobie, ed.
12	PTFS-10	1932	*Tone the Bell Easy*. Dobie, ed.
13	PTFS-11	1933	*Spur-of-the-Cock*. Dobie, ed.
14	ExB-2	1934	*Tall Tales from Texas*. Mody C. Boatright
15	PTFS-12	1935	*Puro Mexicano*. Dobie, ed.
16	ExB-3	1936	*Swing and Turn: Texas Play-Party Games*. William A. Owens
17	PTFS-13	1937	*Straight Texas*. Dobie, ed.
18	PTFS-14	1938	*Coyote Wisdom*. Dobie, ed.
19	PTFS-15	1939	*In the Shadow of History*. Dobie, ed.
20	PTFS-16	1940	*Mustangs and Cow Horses*. Dobie, ed.
21	PTFS-17	1941	*Texian Stomping Grounds*. Dobie, ed.
22	RLS-1 & ExB-4	1942	*My Rambles as East Texas Cowboy, Hunter, Fisherman, Tie-Cutter*. Solomon Alexander Wright

23	RLS-2	1943	*Ed Nichols Rode a Horse*. Ruby Nichols Cutbirth
24	RLS-3	1943	*A Tenderfoot Kid on Gyp Water*. Carl Peters Benedict
25	RLS-4	1943	*A Stove-Up Cowboy's Story*. James Emmit McCauley
26	PTFS-18	1943	*Backwoods to Border*. Mody C. Boatright, ed.
27	PTFS-19	1944	*From Hell to Breakfast*. Boatright, ed.
28	RLS-5	1945	*The Prairie Dog Lawyer*. Charles E. Coombes
29	PTFS-20	1945	*Gib Morgan, Minstrel of the Oil Fields*. Mody C. Boatright
30	P-2	1946	*When the Woods Were Burnt*. Boatright, ed.
31	PTFS-21	1946	*Mexican Border Ballads and Other Lore*. Boatright, ed.
32	ExB-5	1947	*Adventures with a Texas Naturalist*. Roy Bedichek
33	PTFS-22	1948	*The Sky is My Tipi*. Boatright, ed.
34	ExB-6	1949	*Folk Laughter on the American Frontier*. Mody C. Boatright
35	PTFS-23	1950	*Texas Folk Songs*. William A. Owens
36	PTFS-24	1951	*The Healer of Los Olmos and Other Mexican Lore*. Wilson M. Hudson, ed.
37	ExB-7	1952	*The Typical Texan, Biography of an American Myth*. Joseph Leach
38	PTFS-25	1953	*Folk Travelers, Ballads, Tales, and Talk*. Boatright, ed.
39	PTFS-26	1954	*Texas Folk and Folklore*. Boatright, ed.
40	ExB-8	1955	*Tales of Old-Time Texas*. J. Frank Dobie
41	PTFS-27	1956	*Mesquite and Willow*. Boatright, ed.
42	PTFS-28	1957	*Madstones and Twisters*. Boatright, ed.
43	ExB-9	1958	*"With His Pistol in His Hand," A Border Ballad and Its Hero*. Americo Paredes
44	PTFS-29	1959	*and horns on the toads*. Boatright, ed.
45	PTFS-30	1960	*Singers and Storytellers*. Boatright, ed.
46	PTFS-31	1961	*The Golden Log*. Boatright, ed.,
47	PTFS-32	1962	*A Good Tale and a Bonnie Tune*. Boatright, ed.
48	ExB-10	1963	*Folklore of the Oil Industry*. Mody C. Boatright
49	P-3	1964	*Folksong and Folksong Scholarship*. Tristam P. Coffin
50	ExB-11	1964	*Friends of Thunder, Folktales of the Oklahoma Cherokees*. Jack F. Kilpatrick
51	P-4	1965	*Mody Boatright, Secretary and Editor, 1943–1964*. Wilson M. Hudson, ed.
52	PTFS-33	1965	*The Sunny Slopes of Long Ago*. Wilson M. Hudson, ed.
53	PBS-1	1966	*Mirrors, Mice, & Mustaches*. George D. Hendricks
54	ExB-12	1966	*Tales from the Big Thicket*. Francis E. Abernethy
55	P-5	1967	*Eyes on Texas, Fifty Years of Folklore in the Southwest*. Wayland D. Hand
56	PTFS-34	1967	*Tire Shrinker to Dragster*. Hudson, ed.
57	PBS-2	1967	*Pecos Tales*. Paul Patterson
58	PBS-4 & ExB-13	1968	*Deep Like the Rivers, Stories of My Negro Friends*. Martha Emmons
59	PBS-3	1969	*Aunt Puss & Others, Old Days in the Piney Woods*. Emma Wilson Emery
60	PTFS-35	1969	*Hunters & Healers: Folklore Types & Topics*. Hudson, ed.
61	PBS-5	1970	*Texas Folk Medicine, 1,333 Cures, Remedies, Preventives, & Health Practices*. John Q. Anderson, ed.

62	ExB-14	1970	*There Was a King in Ireland . . . Five Tales from Oral Tradition*. Myles Dillon
63	PTFS-36	1971	*Diamond Bessie & The Shepherds*. Hudson, ed.
64	PTFS-37	1972	*Observations & Reflections on Texas Folklore*. Francis Edward Abernethy, ed.
65	SRP-1	1973	*Analytical Index to Publications of the Texas Folklore Society, Volumes 1–36*. James T. Bratcher
66	ExB-15	1973	*Mody Boatright, Folklorist, A Collection of Essays*. Ernest B. Speck, ed.
67	PTFS-38	1974	*The Folklore of Texan Cultures*. Abernethy, ed.
68	PTFS-39	1975	*Some Still Do: Essays on Texas Customs*. Abernethy, ed.
69	PTFS-40	1976	*What's Going On? (In Modern Texas Folklore)*. Abernethy, ed.
70	ExB-16	1977	*Myths & Folktales of the Alabama-Coushatta Indians of Texas*. Howard N. Martin
71	PTFS-41	1978	*Paisanos: A Folklore Miscellany*. Abernethy, ed.
72	PTFS-42	1979	*Built in Texas*. Abernethy, ed.
73	ExB-17	1980	*Mexican Folktales from the Borderland*. Riley Aiken
74	PTFS-43	1981	*Legendary Ladies of Texas*. Abernethy, ed.
75	PTFS-44	1982	*T for Texas: A State Full of Folklore*. Abernethy, ed.
76	ExB-18	1983	*Singin' Texas*. Francis Edward Abernethy
77	PTFS-45	1984	*Folk Art in Texas*. Abernethy, ed.
78	PTFS-46	1985	*Sonovagun Stew*. Abernethy, ed.
79	ExB-19	1986	*Dance Across Texas*. Betty Casey
80	PTFS-47	1987	*Hoein' the Short Rows*. Abernethy, ed.
81	ExB-20	1988	*Mexican-American Folklore*. John O. West
82	PTFS-48	1989	*Texas Toys and Games*. Abernethy, ed.
83	PTFS-49	1990	*The Bounty of Texas*. Abernethy, ed.
84	PTFS-50	1991	*Hecho en Tejas*. Joe S. Graham, ed.
85	PTFS-51	1992	*The Texas Folklore Society: 1909–1943, Vol. I*. Abernethy
86	PTFS-52	1993	*Corners of Texas*. Abernethy, ed.
87	PTFS-53	1994	*The Texas Folklore Society: 1943–1971, Vol. II*. Abernethy
88	ExB-21	1995	*Through Time and the Valley*. John Erickson
89	PTFS-54	1996	*Juneteenth Texas: Essays in African-American Folklore*. Abernethy, Mullen, Governar, eds.
90	PTFS-55	1997	*Between the Cracks of History: Essays on Teaching and Illustrating Folklore*. Abernethy, ed.
91	ExB-22	1998	*The Best of Texas Folk and Folklore 1916–1954*. (Reprint)
92	PTFS-56	1999	*Features and Fillers: Texas Journalists on Texas Folklore*. Jim Harris, ed.
93	PTFS-57	2000	*The Texas Folklore Society: 1971–2000, Vol. III*, Abernethy

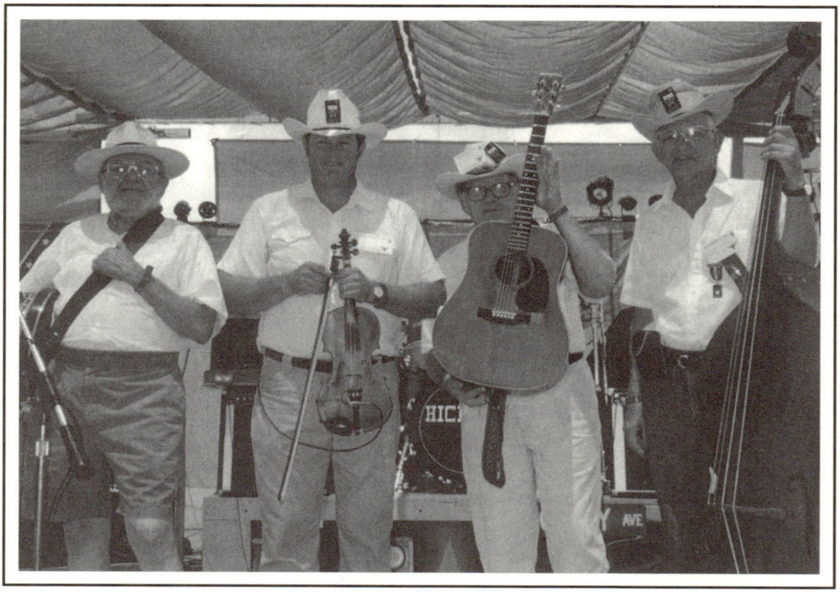

The East Texas String Ensemble, who entertained at TFS meetings over a period of thirty years. LtoR: Tom Nall, Ronnie Wolfe, Stan Alexander, Ab Abernethy

Officers, Directors, and Councilors for 1998. Top row: Tom Crum, Vice President Sylvia Mahoney, R. G. Dean, Secretary-Editor F. E. Abernethy, George Ewing, Henry Wolff. Bottom Row: Margaret Waring, Faye Leeper, President Rollo Newsom, Counselor Bill Stokes, Mary Harris

Certificate of Incorporation with Amendments and By-Laws

The Certificate of Incorporation (Charter No. 243617) designated the Society as a non-profit incorporation. It was signed on February 12, 1968, by John L. Hill, Secretary of State. The text of the original 1968 Certificate as well as the texts of the 1969 and 1989 amended Certificates are as follows:

We, the undersigned natural persons of the age of twenty-one years or more, at least two of whom are citizens of the State of Texas, acting as incorporators of a corporation under the Texas Non-Profit Corporation Act, do hereby adopt the following articles of incorporation for such corporation: ARTICLE ONE: The name of the corporation is THE TEXAS FOLKLORE SOCIETY. ARTICLE TWO: The corporation is a non-profit corporation. ARTICLE THREE: The period of its duration is fifty (50) years. ARTICLE FOUR: The purposes for which it is organized are educational, sociological and scientific, the society in its unincorporated form having been organized at the University of Texas in 1909 and having been an active folklore society since then; the principal aims, purposes and activities of the society are to collect, preserve and study folklore and folk cultures, with especial emphasis on the folklore, folksongs, folktales and folk literature of Texas and the Southwest. ARTICLE FIVE: The street address of the initial registered office of the corporation is English Building 12, University of Texas, Austin, Texas 78712, and the name of its initial registered agent at such address is Wilson M. Hudson. ARTICLE SIX: The number of directors constituting the initial board of directors of the corporation is five, and the names and addresses of the persons who are to serve as the initial directors are: (1) James W. Lee, (2) John O. West, (3) Arthur M. Cory, (4) Wilson M. Hudson, (5) Hermes Nye.

The Articles of Incorporation were amended on May 6, 1969, and signed by Martin Dies, Jr., Secretary of State.

(a) ARTICLE FOUR of the original Articles of Incorporation shall have the additional following provision, to-wit: Said purposes also include the making of distributions to organizations that qualify as exempt organizations under 501 (c)(3) of the Internal Revenue Code of 1954 (or the corresponding provision of any future United States Internal Revenue Law). (b) A new Article to-wit: ARTICLE EIGHT is hereby added to the said Article of Incorporation, to-wit: No part of the net earnings of the corporation shall inure to the benefit of or be distributable to its members, trustees, officers, or other private persons, except that the corporation shall be authorized and empowered to pay reasonable compensation for services rendered and to make payments and distributions in furtherance of the purposes set forth in Article Four of said original Articles of Incorporation, and Article Two hereof. (c) A new Article, to-wit: ARTICLE NINE is added thereto as follows to-wit: No substantial part of the activities of the corporation shall be the carrying on of propaganda, or otherwise attempting to influence legislation, and the corporation shall not participate in, or intervene in (including the publishing or distribution of statements) any political campaign on behalf of any candidate for public office. (d) A new Article, to-wit ARTICLE TEN is added thereto as follows to-wit: Notwithstanding any other provision of these articles, the corporation shall not carry on any other activities not permitted to be carried on (a) by a corporation exempt from Federal income tax under section 501(c)(3) of the Internal Revenue Code of 1954 (or the corresponding provision of any future United States Internal Revenue Law) or (b) by a corporation, contributions to which are deductible under section 170(c)(2) of the Internal Revenue Code of 1954 (or the corresponding provision of any future United States Internal Revenue Law). (e) A new Article, to-wit ARTICLE ELEVEN is added thereto as follows to-wit: Upon the dissolution of the corporation, the Board of Directors shall, after paying or making provision for the payment of all of the liabilities of the corporation, dispose of all of the assets of the corporation exclusively for the purposes of the corporation in such manner, or to such organization or organizations organized and operated exclusively for charitable, educational, religious, or scientific purposes as shall at the time qualify as an exempt organization or organizations under section 501(c)(3) of the Internal Revenue Code of 1954 (or the corresponding provision of any future United State Internal Revenue Law), as the Board of Directors shall determine. Any of such assets not so disposed of shall be disposed of by the Probate of county court of the county in which the principal office of the corporation is then located, exclusively for such purposes or to such organization or organizations as said Court shall determine, which are organized and operated exclusively for such purposes.

On March 25, 1989, the Articles of Incorporation were further amended to make certain provisions for defining and limiting the liability of directors, officers and councilors of the corporation. The important amendment is Article Twelve:

DIRECTORS, OFFICERS AND COUNSILORS [sic!] of the Texas Folklore Society shall not be personally liable to the corporation or its members for monetary damages for acts or omissions in the capacity of such officers, directors or councilors, except liability for (1) An act or omission not in good faith or that involves intentional misconduct or a knowing violation of the law. (2) A transaction from which a director, officer or councilor received an improper benefit, whether or not the benefit resulted from an action taken within the scope of the office of such person. (3) An act or omission for which the liability of a director, officer or councilor is expressly provided for by statute.

ARTICLE THREE. The amendments were adopted in the following manner: The amendments first were adopted and approved by the unanimous vote of the board of directors of the corporation, a quorum being present, on the 24th day of March, 1989, and then by a vote of the membership of the corporation, a quorum being present, and more than two-thirds of the members present having voted in favor thereof, such membership meeting being held on the 25th day of March, 1989.

The amended Articles of Incorporation were filed on March 31 and approved and signed by Secretary of State Jack M. Rains on April 5, 1989.

At the same meeting that the Articles of Incorporation were first approved, the Texas Folklore Society By-Laws were adopted by the membership: April 13, 1968, at Alpine, John O. West, President; Wilson M. Hudson, Secretary-Editor.

ARTICLE 1: Meetings of members, officers and directors shall be held at least once a year at such time, date and place as such respective classes of persons shall select. At present, all such classes of persons hold an annual meeting on or about 11:00 A.M. on the Saturday immediately preceding Easter, at such place as the members have selected on the preceding year. Special meetings of any such classes or persons may be held at any time on the giving of ten days' advance written notice by the President of the Society.

ARTICLE 2: Members shall consist of those persons whose dues are currently paid up. Every member shall be entitled to one vote if present in person. A quorum shall consist of ten or more members present, and three persons present and voting shall constitute a quorum for meetings of the officers and of the Board of Directors.

ARTICLE 3: The members at their annual meeting shall select the necessary officers and directors. Officers shall serve a term of one year each. There shall be five voting directors, one to serve a term of one year, two a term of two years each, and two to serve a term of three years each. A "year" in this paragraph means from one Easter to the next.

If any officer or director is unable or unwilling to serve, the President shall appoint a member of the Society to fill the unexpired term of such office or position.

The officers of the Society shall consist of a President, one or more Vice-Presidents, a Secretary, and Editor whose duties shall be combined with those of the Secretary, the position to be henceforth known as Secretary-Editor, a Treasurer, and such other officers as the members shall from time to time designate.

The members may select annually a number of Councillors, their number and duties to be such as the members shall designate.

ARTICLE FOUR: The President shall be in general charge of the affairs of the Society. The Vice-President shall have such duties as shall be designated by the members, and shall preside at appropriate meetings in the absence of the President. The Secretary-Editor shall keep the seal of the Society and maintain a minute book and have such other duties as shall be designated by the members. The Treasurer shall be in charge of the financial affairs of the Society, shall keep an accurate set of financial records for the Society and make such financial reports and returns as shall be required by law: He shall also maintain a bank account in the name of the Society, and the signature of the Treasurer and of one other officer, to be designated by the members, shall be required on all checks or documents of withdrawal: He shall also have such other duties as shall be designated by the members.

Any other officers of the Society shall have such duties as shall be designated by the members.

The President shall be a non-voting member of the Board of Directors and shall be Chairman of the Board of Directors. The Secretary-Editor shall be a non-voting member of the Board of Directors.

ARTICLE 5: These by-laws may be amended by the members at any annual meeting.

ARTICLE 6: The offices of the Society shall be at Parlin Hall, University of Texas, Austin, Texas, or at such other place as the members shall designate.

ARTICLE 7: The corporate and fiscal year shall be from January 1st of one year to January 1st of the following year, beginning with January 1st, 1968.

ARTICLE 8: All official decisions of meetings of the members, or of the officers, or of the Board of Directors, shall be by Majority vote of those present and voting.

Index

Page references in *italics* refer to photographs and illustrations.

The abbreviation "TFS" refers to the Texas Folklore Society.

Secretary-Editor Francis E. Abernethy, when he first took office in 1972, and twenty-seven years later, in 1999.